History's Women
The Unsung Heroines

History's Women
The Unsung Heroines

Patricia R. Chadwick

History's Women
The Unsung Heroines

Dedication

To my husband, John, who has always given me the freedom to be myself and encouraged me to become all that God intended me to be.

Table of Contents

Acknowledgements

History has always been one of my great loves. I've spent many years with my nose in a book, learning all I could about people who lived in by-gone days. The more I studied, however, the more I became aware of the fact that the achievements of women throughout history were sorely under-represented.

Thus began my quest to find out more about the lives of women who made a difference in their worlds. As I searched the halls of history for the achievements of women, I discovered that women throughout history held a variety of important positions. I encountered women lawyers, scientists, doctors, ministers, authors, artists, singers, social reformers, and rulers that I'd never heard about. All these women, from mothers to queens, made a difference in their spheres of influence.

The result of this journey through women's history led me to start a website called *History's Women*, found at http://www.historyswomen.com. *History's Women* is an online magazine highlighting the extraordinary achievements of women throughout history and recognizing the obstacles they've had to overcome in order to reach their goals. I send out a weekly newsletter with a new profile of a great woman every week. This book is an outgrowth of the ministry of **History's Women Website**. It is a labor of love and my contribution to women across the globe, helping them realize their great heritage.

I'd like to thank my family for the love and support they've shown me over the past year as I've taken on this project. They've put up with many "take out" meals, extra chores, and countless hours with mom at the computer. I'd also like to thank my mother, Alice Brasky, for being a great role model and a wonderful mother. She is truly one of this world's unsung heroines.

Finally, I'd like to thank Alison Rivera of Dezigns By Ali (www.dezignsbyali.com) for creating the cover and all the artwork and graphics for the entire book.

Introduction

Throughout the ages, the majority of historians have overlooked the achievements of women. When one looks back throughout history, whether secular or Christian, they will find the deeds of great men displayed in written accounts with great detail. To find out the effects women had on society, one will have to dig much deeper.

It wasn't until the later part of the nineteenth century that volumes on the contributions of women to society began to appear in any significant proportion. Up until this time, while the written record was not silent on the achievements of women, the volumes detailing the lives of great women were few.

Though their contributions are not recorded in many history books, from the beginning of time, women have had a profound influence on the worlds in which they lived. God has used women throughout history in a variety of ways. From the earliest of times lived women who ruled nations, led armies, wrote books and songs, performed mighty deeds of valor, and worked unceasingly to improve society. Without the contributions of godly women throughout the ages, the world would be a different place today.

While, if you search hard enough, you will be able to find records of these great women in the annals of history, it wasn't until the twentieth century that volumes recording the deeds of women began appearing in greater numbers. A resurgence of interest in women's history took place in the later part of the twentieth century, leading numerous women authors to research the contribution that women have made to the world. It was during this time frame that volumes began appearing under the topic of Woman Studies.

In today's world, thankfully, proper credit is now being given to women who have made great achievements. The impact that women have had on the world in days gone by, as well as in this present age, are now being recognized and recorded. This book is just the beginning. My hope is that you will begin on your own journey and discover for yourself the legacy of women who changed the worlds in which they lived. May these profiles of great women encourage all women, everywhere, to strive to achieve their very best and to make an impact on their world.

1

Early America

Pocahontas
Indian Princess

Mary Chilton Winslow
Pilgrim

Sarah Bache
Daughter of Benjamin Franklin

Molly Pitcher
Revolutionary War Hero

Emily Geiger

Patricia R. Chadwick

The Daring Messenger

Betsy Ross
America's First Flag

Mary Youngs Pickersgill
Maker of the
"Star Spangled Banner"

Varina Anne Davis
Daughter of the Confederacy

Pocahontas
Indian Princess

Pocahontas, an Indian princess of Virginia, was born in 1595, the daughter of chief Powhatan. She is well known for her courage and compassion as showed in her friendship toward the English colonists of Jamestown.

According to legend, Captain John Smith was taken prisoner, and it was decided to put him to death. His head was laid upon a stone, and the Indians were brandishing their clubs preparing to beat him to death, when Pocahontas, a mere 12 years of age, threw herself upon the captive's body, and pleaded with her father to spare his life. Powhatan relented and Smith's life was spared.

When Smith returned to Jamestown, he sent presents to Pocahontas and her father; and after this, according to Smith's narrative, Pocahontas "with her wild train visited Jamestown as freely as her father's habitation."

Because of her friendship toward the colonists and Captain Smith, Pocahontas once again showed great courage. In 1609 Pocahontas passed through the woods in the night to inform Smith of a plot formed by her father to destroy him. Because of this warning, Smith was able to prepare and protect himself from harm.

16

In 1612 she was kidnapped, by order of Governor Thomas Dale, and held for ransom, to be paid in corn by Chief Powhatan. During this time, Pocahontas became a Christian and was baptized, being given the Christian name of Rebecca. It was also during this imprisonment that Pocahontas became acquainted with John Rolfe, who sought her hand in marriage. Sir Thomas Dale and Chief Powhatan gave consent and they were married at Jamestown in April 1613. This union brought a peace of many years duration between the English and the Indians (King, *Woman*, p. 265).

In 1616 she accompanied Governor Dale to England, where she was an object of great interest to all classes of people, and was presented at court. As Pocahontas and John Rolfe were preparing to leave England, she suddenly became ill with pneumonia. Pocahontas died in Gravesend, England in March 1617, leaving behind her husband and one son, Thomas Rolfe.

Pocahontas was a woman of courage and compassion. Largely due to her intervention, the colony of Jamestown was able to thrive and succeed in the New World.

Mary Chilton Winslow
Pilgrim

Mary Chilton Winslow has the distinction of being the first, woman to step foot on Plymouth Rock as the Pilgrims descended from the Mayflower after crossing the Atlantic in 1620.

Mary was born sometime around 1608, probably in England. She was the daughter of James Chilton and Susanna Furner, who were married before the year 1587 in England. Not much is known about Mary's heritage, but it appears that her father was the son of Lionel Chilton and her mother was likely the daughter of Francis and Isabelle Furner. Both parents were "Separatists" or "Pilgrims" which was a religious group that were dissenters from the Church of England.

In the early 1600's many of the English began to question the teachings of the Church of England or Anglican Church. Henry VIII had founded the Church of England when he separated from the Catholic Church in order to get a divorce from Catherine of Aragon to marry Anne Bolyen. Some of these individuals chose to remain members of the Church of England and "purify" it from within and were called "Puritans". A more radical group believed that the Church of England was too corrupt to be salvaged and these individuals separated from the church and were nicknamed "Separatists". These Separatists were persecuted by the English monarchy and even by the Puritans within the Church of England. Many fled to Holland where their religious views were tolerated. This same group also soon became known as "Pilgrims", because they were forced to wander from their native land looking for religious freedom.

Though it has been widely disputed, it is now believed by most that the Chilton family was a part of the group of Separatists that fled to Leyden, Holland. It is recorded that in 1619, Mary and her father, James Chilton were attacked by a group of rock throwing boys in Leyden, Holland. Therefore it appears that her parents were indeed Separatists.

While life in Holland was easier for the Pilgrims than a life of persecution in England, it was still difficult for the Separatists to make a living. Most of the group had been farmers in England and upon moving to Holland they had to learn new skills to survive in an urban land that afforded them only a meager income. Besides being hard to eke out a living, the adults of this group felt that their children were becoming too immersed in the Dutch culture and were slipping away from their faith.

Because of this, the Pilgrims decided to leave Holland. The leaders of the group entered an agreement with a group of "Adventurers" or businessmen in England who wanted to profit off those interested in beginning a new life in the New World. The agreement was made that in exchange for their passage; the Pilgrims would give the Adventurers a percentage of their first harvest. Along with the Pilgrims, the Adventurers also paid the passage of a number of people who were going to America for financial gain. The Pilgrims called these people "Strangers". The first group Pilgrims set sail on the

Mayflower in 1620. Mary Chilton and her family were on this ship. The total number of Pilgrims aboard the Mayflower was 102.

The ship was headed to the Jamestown Colony, Virginia, but missed its mark, whether by mistake or planning. The Mayflower arrived at Cape Cod in November of 1620. James Chilton, who was one of the oldest of the Mayflower passengers, died on December 18, 1620 while the Mayflower was docked in Provincetown Harbor. There is no record as to whether he was buried.

The leaders aboard the Mayflower decided not to stay at Cape Cod and continued down the coast to Plymouth where the passengers founded a new colony. According to tradition Mary Chilton raced John Alden to the front of the launch that was bringing the Mayflower passengers ashore. She stepped off the boat and was the first woman to set foot on Plymouth Rock. The painting, "The Landing of the Pilgrims", by Henry Bacon, reflects this tradition. The first winter that the Pilgrims spent in Plymouth was an extremely hard one with grave consequences. Nearly half of the passengers that made it across the Atlantic died in and epidemic referred to as "The First Sickness", including Mary's mother. This left the thirteen-year-old Mary an orphan. After the death of her mother, it is believed that Mary lived for the next few years with the family of Miles Standish or John Alden.

In 1621, John Winslow, brother of Mayflower passenger Edward Winslow, came to America on the "Fortune". Mary and John met and were married sometime before 1627, probably in July of 1623. They had ten children together: John, Susanna, Mary Edward, Sarah, Samuel, Joseph, Isaac, an unnamed child who died young, and Benjamin. The youngest child, Benjamin, is the only child listed in the Plymouth records.

Sometime after the birth of their last child, the Winslow family moved to Boston where John became a successful merchant and ship owner. It was here that they both died, John in 1674 and Mary in 1679. Mary was the only female passenger from the Mayflower who left a will.

Sarah Franklin Bache
Daughter of Benjamin Franklin

One of the most popular women of her day in her native city was Sarah Franklin. She was born in 1744 the daughter of Benjamin and Deborah Read Franklin in the city of Philadelphia. Carefully educated by her father, she was said to be as broadly educated as any woman in the Colony. As a girl, she is said to have been plain, almost ugly, but with a sense of humor and a wittiness which, combined with her good nature and kindness, make her generally popular.

Of her girlhood there is little to tell. She lived a rather uneventful life until she was twenty years old. At this time her father was sent to England in a representative capacity. The incident leading up to this was the first introduction Sarah had to politics, a subject that remained a keen interest of hers throughout her life.

Some of Miss Franklin's letters to her father during his absence in England have been preserved and give insight into the strong feeling that agitated the American people of the day. They also show us the intimacy between father and daughter.

Sarah was married in October 1767 to Richard Bache, a merchant of Philadelphia, who had come to the colony several years before from Yorkshire, England. For several years, Mr.

and Mrs. Bach lived with Deborah Franklin, while Benjamin was in England. They stayed with her until she died of paralysis in December 1774, while her father was still in England as agent of the Province of Pennsylvania. Sarah was called upon to take the place of her mother in the family as homemaker before and during the Revolution.

Sarah Franklin Bach was well known for her own patriotism and public spirit. She was useful to both her family and her country in a time of personal and national turmoil. Sarah developed cancer in 1807 and passed away in October, 1808 at the age of sixty-four.

Molly Pitcher
Revolutionary War Hero

Mary Ludwig Hays was the daughter of John George Ludwig a New Jersey Dairy farmer. She was born on October 13, 1744, near Trenton New Jersey. When Mary or "Molly", as she was nicknamed, was old enough to work, at the tender age of thirteen, she was employed as a house servant at Carlisle, Pennsylvania, in the family of General William Irvine. In the summer of 1769, when she was twenty-five years of age, Molly married to John Hays, a barber by trade. Soon after they were married, John enlisted in Proctor's First Pennsylvania Artillery. Molly, not wanting to be separated from her beloved husband, decided to go with him when he went to war.

It was not unusual, during the American Revolution, for wives to follow their husbands to war. Generally, the wives of private soldiers would follow the armies into the field as laundry women. The women were assigned lodgings and wagons carried them from place to place.

The story of the battle of Monmouth is not complete without the telling of the story of Molly Hays. The battle of Monmouth was fought June 28, 1778 under the directive of General Washington while the enemy troops were commanded by General Clinton. The enemy had attacked the American regiment, which lined a hedgerow across an open field. Some American artillery took post on a hill in the rear of this fence, but the British cavalry had a large body of infantry, skilled in the use of the bayonet, and they charged upon the Americans and broke their ranks. It is for her part in this portion of the battle that Molly is remembered. It is here that during this she displayed the great courage and presence of mind, for which she is remembered.

Molly's husband, John, was in charge of firing one of the cannons. The day was sweltering and the artillerymen were suffering from the heat. Molly was not far away from watching the fight and could see that the men were thirsty. She obtained a bucket - or "pitcher" - and began to bring water, for them from a neighboring spring. Whenever the men were thirsty, they would call out, "Molly - pitcher." And she would bring them the water they so desperately needed. This is how she became well known by the name of Molly Pitcher. In fact, "Molly Pitcher" became the nickname for all women who performed the duty of carrying water to the troops during the American Revolutionary War (Wheeler, *Daughters of Destiny*, p. 181).

The story doesn't end here. While thus engaged, Molly saw her dear husband fall in battle. She ran to his aid, but he was dead when she reached him. Just then, poor Molly heard an officer order the gun removed because there was no one else to take his place. Molly's patriotism rose to the surface, even in her grief. Facing the officer, she asked to be allowed to take her husband's place. Her request, though unusual, was granted, and she handled the job with skill and courage. She attended the cannon until the battle was won.

Patricia R. Chadwick

Emily Geiger
Daring Messenger

While we find many stories of men performing heroic deeds throughout history of America, we find very few records of women serving their country. This, however, does not mean that women did not serve their country. There are accounts of women who have nobly performed their patriotic duty. One of those women was Emily Geiger.

The bearing of important dispatches through an enemy's country is an endeavor that always requires both courage and concentration. Miss Emily Geiger performed such an exploit during the American Revolution, under difficult circumstances.

General Nathaniel Greene's troops had retreated before Lord Rawdon. When Greene passed Broad river, he was wanted to send an order to General Thomas Sumter to join him so that they might attack Lord Rawdon, who had divided his force. General Greene, however, could find no man in that part of the state who was bold enough to undertake so dangerous a mission.

The country to be passed through for many miles was full of the enemy, who on every occasion that offered drenched their hands in the blood of their foes. At length, Emily Geiger presented herself to General Greene, and proposed to act as his messenger.

Emily was the daughter of John and Emily Murphy Geiger. Due to his ill health, her father could not go to the battlefield, making Emily extremely eager to serve her country in some way.

The general, both surprised and delighted, consented to her proposal. He quickly wrote a letter and at the same time communicated the contents of it verbally, to be told to Sumter in case of accidents and/or capture.

Emily pursued her journey on horseback on a sidesaddle. She traveled under the guise of being on her way to her Uncle Jacob's house many miles away. But on the second day Lord Rawdon's scouts near the Congaree River intercepted her. Coming from the direction of Greene's army and not being able to tell an untruth without blushing, Emily was suspected and confined to a room.

The officer sent for an old matron to search her for papers. Emily immediately sought to destroy the letter. As soon as the door was closed and she found herself alone, she ate up the letter, piece by piece. After a while, Mrs. Hogabook, the matron arrived. She carefully searched Emily, but nothing was found of a suspicious nature about the prisoner and Emily would disclose nothing. Suspicion being then relieved, the officer commanding the scouts apologized for the error and allowed her to leave, giving her an escort to her uncle's home.

The next day, Emily took a somewhat roundabout route to avoid further detentions. She continued on her journey and arrived safely. Emily told the general of her adventure and delivered Greene's verbal message to Sumter, who, soon after, joined the main army at Orangeburgh (Wheeler, *Daughters of Destiny,* p. 180).

Betsy Ross
Maker of America's First Flag

There has been much controversy over the years as to who indeed make the first American Flag. While attempts have been made to disprove it, it is generally accepted by most Americans that the first American Flag was fashioned by Betsy Ross. While there is no historical record of Mrs. Ross being commissioned to made the first flag, there is a strong verbal record, handed down from generation to generation, beginning with Betsy's own family.

Betsy Ross was born Elizabeth Griscom in Philadelphia, Pennsylvania on January 1, 1752, the seventh daughter, and eighth child of the seventeen children born to Samuel and Rebecca James Griscom. Her grandfather, Andrew Griscom emigrated from England to New Jersey in 1680 and later became aquatinted with William Penn and helped him to found the city of Philadelphia, moving there to be a part of William Penn's Quaker community dubbed the "holy experiment". Andrew was a respected carpenter, as was his son. It is commonly accepted that Betsy's father, Samuel assisted in the construction of Independence Hall. Her mother, Rebecca James, was the daughter of a wealthy importer.

Being Quakers, the Griscom's strongly believed in the equality of women. Because of this, they provided their children, including their daughters, with a good education. In her youth Betsy attended Rebecca Jones School for Quakers, which had been chartered by William Penn. Along with her education, she was taught needlework at home, becoming very skillful. As a teenager, she was an apprentice at an upholstery shop owned by William Webster. While today we think of upholsterers primarily as sofa-makers/recoverers, etc., in colonial times they performed all manner of sewing jobs, including flag making.

Betsy was an attractive girl and had many suitors. But it was while working in the upholsterer's shop that Betsy met and fell in love with another apprentice, John Ross, who was the son of an Episcopal assistant rector at Christ Church. At twenty-one, Betsy decided to marry John Ross, against the wishes of her parents. Though he was a Christian, Ross was not a Quaker and Betsy was warned not to marry "out of the meeting", meaning she was not to marry a man other than another Quaker. Quakers frowned on inter-denominational marriages, and the penalty for such unions was expulsion - being emotionally and economically cut off from both family and meetinghouse.

Regardless of the consequences, in November of 1773, John and Betsy secretly rowed across the Delaware River in the dark so they could be married in New Jersey. When the news of the marriage reached her parents, the Griscom's disowned Betsy. In addition, the Quakers publicly excommunicated her. Despite all this, the couple was happy and found a spiritual home at Christ Church.

In 1774, the Rosses opened their own upholstery business at Arch Street. By this time, the rebellion against England was gaining momentum, and Betsy and John were strong American patriots and supporters of colonial rights. Ross' uncle, George Ross, began recruiting male Philadelphians for a militia, and John became a guard of the ammunition stores along the Delaware River near his home. In mid-January 1776, John Ross was mortally wounded when the gunpowder he was guarding exploded. While the young Betsy did her best to nurse him back to health, John died on January 21, 1776.

Betsy became a widow at age twenty-four, after just three years of marriage. This was a trying time for the young girl. Not only was she widowed, but she had also been cut-off from her family because of their choice to marry outside her denomination. But instead of attempting to return to her father's house, Betsy decided to continue their upholstering business, maintaining her independence and her strong colonial sympathies.

Tradition holds that about five months later, in June of 1776, Betsy Ross received a visit from a secret committee sent by the Continental Congress that was authorized to design a flag for the nation-to-be. The committee included George Washington, commander-in-chief of the colonial army, Col. George Ross, Betsy's uncle by marriage, and Robert Morris, a wealthy businessman. They asked that Betsy make the flag according to a rough drawing they carried with them. She consented to attempt the work after suggesting some slight changes, one being a star of five-points instead of six, Washington redrew the flag design in pencil in her back parlor and Betsy spent the next few days sewing the flag in her home (James, *Notable Women*, p. 198).

When she was finished, she called for the committee who

took it to the State House where Congress approved the design. While the committee had gone to other seamstresses, Betsy Ross' flag is the one the Continental Congress decided upon, and they gave her a standing order. She continued making flags for the United States Government for the next fifty years.

Betsy Ross was a mere 25 when she sewed the country's first flag. She was a fine young woman, who was well educated and had a practical knowledge of science and medicine. She was also a zealous patriot for the American cause, continuing to stand up for colonial rights to the extent that when British soldiers took over her house during their occupation of Philadelphia in 1777, they nicknamed her "The Little Rebel".

In late 1777, Betsy remarried. Her new husband, Joseph Ashburn, had been a suitor of hers from her youth. Though she gave birth to two daughters from this marriage, she only had a few years with Joseph. A soldier with the American forces, the British took him prisoner in 1781. For several long months, Betsy went without news of her husband, but kept herself busy with her business, her daughters, and her service to the army (making quilts and blankets). She also left Christ Church and joined a new group of Quakers called Free Quakers, that supported the Revolution. They were a great help to Betsy during this trying period.

In March of 1782, Joseph Ashburn died in an English prison. Upon his release from the same prison, a friend and fellow prisoner, John Claypool, called on Betsy to deliver a farewell message from her late husband. Ironically, Claypool had also courted Betsy before her marriage to John Ross and within a year, on May 8, 1783, they were married.

The Claypool's had five daughters and a full life. Along with John's job with the U.S. Customs House, they were busy running the upholstery business, raising their family, and attending Free Quaker meetings. However, around 1800, John Claypool suffered a devastating stroke requiring almost constant nursing. He lived for 17 years and died at age 65 in August 1817.

Betsy Ross led a full life, giving her life to her family, her work, and her service to her country. In 1827 Betsy retired from the upholstery shop, leaving it to one of her daughters. She lived with different children during the next 9 years, continuing to sew, but this time for her family. She went totally blind in 1835 and died on January 30, 1836.

Patricia R. Chadwick

Mary Youngs Pickersgill
Maker of the "Star Spangled Banner"

While many know the story behind Francis Scott Key penning the beloved "Star Spangle Banner", not many know the story of the flag that was flown at Fort McHenry that inspired the Key to write the words that would become the National Anthem of the United States of America. This flag was created by Mary Young Pickersgill.

Mary Young Pickersgill was born in 1776 in Philadelphia, Pennsylvania, during the difficult period of the Revolutionary War. Her family moved to Lebanon, Pennsylvania during the war and later to Baltimore. There she was married and was widowed.

Mary took up the trade of flag making, needing to support herself and her daughter. She became quite skillful at the trade and became well known as a flag maker. Therefore, during another critical time in U.S. History, she was selected to make the flag for Fort McHenry. In 1813, Major George Armistead hired Mary Young Pickersgill to sew a flag with 15 stars and 15 stripes, the number of states then in the Union. Anticipating an attack on Fort McHenry by the British during the War of 1812, Major Armistead asked that the flag be made extra large so that it would be plainly visible to the English Fleet. He had also hoped the large flag would lift the spirits of the

Baltimoreans, allowing them to see this flag fly in defiance of the British.

Mary and her daughter Caroline, then only a mere 13 years old, accomplished the task in six weeks. She took great care to make sure the flag was well constructed. The entire flag was sewn by hand with flat felled seams and tight stitching, so it would not come apart in the wind. It required four hundred yards of wool material and the finished flag measured 30 by 42 feet. The flag had to be assembled in a nearby malt house, because there was no other place large enough to assemble it.

This flag was used as the garrison flag of Fort McHenry during the British siege of the fort during the War of 1812. When Francis Scott Key saw the flag from a ship eight miles down the Patapsco River on September 14, 1814, the flag was still waving in the breeze after twenty-five hours of heavy bombardment by the British. The British were very discouraged to see it still there, but Key was inspired to write the poem that became our National Anthem.

Patricia R. Chadwick

Varina Anne Davis
Daughter of the Confederacy

Varina Anne Davis, daughter of Mr. and Mrs. Jefferson Davis, was born in 1865 during the last year of the Civil War in the Confederate White House. Her father was the President of the Confederate States at the time of her birth. She was named for her mother and was the youngest of the Davis children. She was called "Winnie" for most of her life; a pet name Jefferson had first given his wife and then his daughter. According to what she was told as a child, "Winnie" was an Indian name meaning "bright or sunny".

When the Civil War was finally over, President Davis became a prisoner. Baby Winnie was the only one of the children allowed to accompany Mrs. Davis on her visit to the prison to see her husband. Soon after this, Winnie was sent to visit relatives in Canada, where she remained until Mr. Davis was settled in Memphis, Tennessee.

Winnie received most of her early education at home from her mother in the post-Civil War years. At the age of twelve, Winnie was taken to Europe, where she was enrolled in a boarding school in Karlsruhe, Germany. Here she received a thorough education. Afterwards, she spent some time in Paris, France, to finish her social education and was then she was ready to take a leading role in the intellectual and social society among the people of the South. Winnie's beauty and grace and her kind-hearted manner made her a distinguished favorite in both the North and the South. Soon after her return to America, while on a visit to Atlanta, she was introduced by General John B. Gordon as "The Daughter of the Confederacy" and this title clung to her for all time (King, *Woman*, p. 467).

Winnie showed much skill in the arts. She was a fine painter and skilled musician. She had also inherited her mother's literary interests and published several books under the name of Varina Anne Jefferson Davis. Some of the titles were "An Irish Knight of the Seventeenth Century", "The Veiled Doctor", and "Foreign Education for American Girls".

Winnie lived with her parents during most of the 1880's and accompanied her father to many public functions. At one point, Winnie was engaged to Alfred C. Wilkinson, a Syracuse, New York attorney, whose grandfather had been a leading abolitionist. While their romance lasted five years, they finally succumbed to public outcry against their union.

In 1891, Winnie moved to New York City to continue her literary career. Later on, she bought a beautiful home at Beuvoir, Mississippi, but the closing years of her life were largely spent in travel.

Varina Anne Davis died on September 18, 1898 after an illness of several weeks. It is believed that on a trip to Rhode Island she contracted "malarial gastritis". The funeral services were held in Richmond, Virginia and her body was laid to rest beside that of her father in Hollywood Cemetery. In keeping with her status among ex-Confederates, Winnie was buried with full military honors.

2

Catherine of Aragon –
First Wife of Henry VIII

Martha Washington
The "First" First Lady

Emma Hart Willard
Founder of the First Permanent Female Seminary

Ada Byron Lovelace
First Computer Programmer

40

Belva Lockwood
Pioneer Woman Lawyer

Antoinette Brown Blackwell
First Ordained Woman Minister in America

Elizabeth Blackwell
First Woman to Receive an M.D. Degree

Lucy Webb Hayes
First Temperance First Lady

Francis Folsom Cleveland
First White House Bride

Baroness Burdett-Coutts
*First Woman to Receive the Title of Baroness for
Her Good Works*

Amelia Earhart
First Woman to Fly Solo Across the Atlantic

Catherine of Aragon
First Wife of Henry VIII

Catherine of Aragon, fourth daughter of Ferdinand and Isabella, king and queen of Aragon and Castile, which is now modern day Spain, was born December 15, 1485. Married in 1501, when scarcely sixteen, to Arthur, Prince of Wales, son of Henry VII, she was left a widow on April 2, 1502. On June 25 of that same year she was betrothed to her brother-in-law, Henry, then only eleven years old. The pope's dispensation enabling such near relatives to marry was obtained in 1504, and the marriage took place in June 1509, seven weeks after Henry's accession to the crown as Henry VIII.

The queen, by her manners, good sense, and superior endowments, managed to maintain the affection of this fickle king for nearly twenty years. She was devoted to literature and was the patroness of literary men. She bore several children, but all of them, excepting a daughter, afterwards Queen Mary, died in their infancy. Scruples, real or pretended, at length arose in the mind of Henry concerning the legality of their union, and they were powerfully enforced by his passion for Anne Boleyn.

In 1527, he resolved to obtain a divorce from Catherine on the grounds that their marriage was contrary to divine laws. Pope Clement VII seemed at first disposed to listen to Henry's application, but overawed by Charles V., emperor of Germany and nephew of Catharine, he caused the negotiations to be so prolonged that Henry became very impatient. Catherine conducted herself with gentleness, yet firmness, in this trying ordeal.

Being tired of waiting, Henry soon threw off his submission to the court of Rome and declared himself the head of the Church of England. As head of the Church, he had his marriage formally annulled by Archbishop Crammer in 1532.

Catherine took up her residency at Ampthill in Bedfordshire, and afterwards at Kimbolton Castle, in Huntingdonshire. She employed herself chiefly in religious duties, bearing her lot in life with silent resignation and dignity. She died in January 1536.

Martha Washington
The "First" First Lady

Martha Washington was born at Chestnut Grove in the county of New Kent, Virginia on June 2, 1731. She was the daughter of John Dandridge and Frances Jones. Martha was the eldest of 9 children. She enjoyed riding horses, gardening, sewing, playing the spinet and dancing. Her father saw that she received a fair education in basic mathematics; reading and writing...something girls primarily did not receive at the time.

At the age of seventeen, she married Col. Daniel Parke Custis, twenty years her senior. They lived in his estate called White House and ran his extensive estate. She had four children by this union: a daughter Frances, who died in infancy, a son named Daniel, whose early death is supposed to have hastened his father's death; Martha (nicknamed Patsy), who died in 1770 as a young woman, and John, who perished in the service of his country, at the siege of Yorktown at the age of 27.

After the death of her first son, Mrs. Custis was left a young widow with great wealth. Martha was an extraordinary woman and her early education proved quite helpful in running the estate left in her care. Her husband's former business manager stayed on to help with the operation of the plantation and she consulted with lawyers when she felt it was necessary.

In 1759 she married George Washington, then a colonel in the colonial service. The new family consisted of George, Martha, Patsy, and John who soon after the marriage made their home at George's estate, Mount Vernon, on the Potomac River. Even though Martha remained at Mount Vernon when George went to Philadelphia as a delegate to the Second Continental Congress, she frequently accompanied him to his headquarters during the war years. She spent the winter of 1775 at his headquarters in Cambridge, Massachusetts, and in the spring of 1776 she accompanied him to New York. In the spring of 1777 she arrived at his headquarters in Morristown, New Jersey, but she returned to Mount Vernon for the summer. The next winter she joined her husband at Valley Forge, and later she stayed with him during campaigns in New Jersey, New York, Pennsylvania, and Maryland. Martha was a very loving mother and grandmother. Because of the untimely death of her son the Washington's raised two of their four grandchildren, Eleanor Parke Custis (Nelly) and George Washington Parke Custis (called Wash or Tub) at Mount Vernon. Even after her sons widow remarried, the two children stayed on at Mount Vernon under their care.

After General Washington's election to the presidency of the United States in 1787, Mrs. Washington became the new country's "first" First Lady. She moved to New York City, the young nation's first capital with George, along with her two grandchildren. She performed the duties of this position with dignity and ease, becoming well known for her hospitality. Even after the retirement of President Washington, Martha still continued her unbounded generosity.

In December 1799, George Washington died

unexpectedly. Martha was too grief-stricken even to attend the funeral. It is to be noted here that George's will ordered the freedom of half of his slaves, leaving the old and the young to remain. Martha freed them all in 1800. Her own health was deteriorating and in March of 1802, sensing her death, she made a will. She then burned all her letters she and her husband had written to one another over the years, except for two.

Martha is an exquisite example of dignity, grace, and marked ability. She not only ran her home and estate with loving, capable hands, but she fulfilled her role as First Lady with equal ability and generosity.

Patricia R. Chadwick

Emma Willard Hart
Founder of the First Female Seminary

The inscription of the statue at "Sage Hall", Troy, NY reads:

IN HONOR OF EMMA HART WILLARD, WHO ON THIS
SPOT ESTABLISHED, A.D., 1821, THE FIRST
PERMANENT SEMINARY IN AMERICA FOR THE
ADVANCED EDUCATION OF WOMEN. ERECTED BY
HER PUPILS AND FRIENDS, A.D. 1895.

HER MOST ENDURING MONUMENT,
THE GRATITUDE OF EDUCATED WOMEN.

Emma Hart Willard was a pioneer educator of women who founded the first permanent female seminary in America. In 1821 she opened the Troy Female Seminary, one of the most influential schools in America, pioneering in the teaching of science, mathematics, and social studies to young women (King, *Woman,* p. 459).

Emma Hart Willard was born on February 23, 1787 to Samuel and Lydia Hinsdale Hart on a farm in Berlin, Connecticut. She was the sixteenth of seventeen children; her father having been previously married, she was his sixteenth and her mother's ninth child.

47

Emma's father was a liberal thinker and though it was out of the ordinary for a girl to be educated, he encouraged her to disregard the norms of the day and to seek an education. Because of this support, she began to acquire an education that was out of the ordinary for girls. Emma was mostly self-taught. At the age of thirteen she had taught herself geometry and at fourteen she would rise at 4:00 in the morning to study the stars in the winter sky. In 1802 she took a significant step and enrolled in the Berlin Academy, her first school. She progressed so rapidly in this environment that soon she was teaching the younger children and in 1806 she took charge of the school for the entire winter term. Clearly having a natural appetite for learning, Emma also attended classes in Hartford during these years and began exploring the possibility of beginning a school for women beyond the confines of their immediate communities.

At the age of twenty she took a job as an assistant at the academy in Westfield, Massachusetts and that summer she went to Middlebury, Vermont to become the principle of the female academy there. It was here that she met Dr. John Willard, a local physician and supporter of female education. They were married on August 10, 1809, when Emma was twenty-two years old and John was fifty.

When she became acquainted with a nephew of Dr. Willard's, who stayed in their home while he attended Middlebury College, she also became acquainted with his books. It was then that she truly began to realize the intellectual deprivation that was the lot of American women and took to heart the vast differences in educational opportunities open to men and to women. She proceeded to study her nephew's textbooks and soon mastered such subjects as geometry and philosophy, preparing her for a larger work.

In 1814, when Dr. Willard suffered financial losses, Emma opened a boarding school in her own home. She called the school the Middlebury Female Seminary, and here she intended to remedy some of the educational disadvantages of young women. Since she was not allowed to attend classes at Middlebury College, she taught herself mathematics and physical science, subjects previously closed to female students, so that she could teach them to the girls in her school. By doing this she proved that she could teach and that young women could learn and master the classical and scientific studies that were previously only taught to men.

In 1818, she sent a plan for a female seminary to the Governor of the neighboring state of New York. Governor Clinton recommended the plan to the Legislature and for the first time the equal rights of women in education were endorsed in legislative halls. A female academy was started at Waterford and was afterwards moved to Troy, New York. The school was an immediate success, even before the first public high schools for girls were opened in New York and Boston in 1826. Emma introduced science courses to her students that were more advanced than those available at many men's colleges and was establishing a serious course of study for women that was dynamic and deserving of respect. Mrs. Willard remained the head of the Troy Female Seminary until 1838 when she turned over the reigns of the school to her son, John Hart Willard and daughter-in-law Sarah Lucretia Hudson.

From 1845 until her death, Emma remained close to the

Troy Female Seminary as an adviser, teacher, speaker, and friend. Emma Hart Willard died at Troy in 1870 when she was eighty-four years old. In 1895 the Troy Female Seminary was renamed Emma Willard School in her honor. Emma Willard School still exists today as a college-preparatory boarding and day school for girls in grades 9-12 and for the post-graduate year, boasting a rigorous academic program enhanced by visual and performing arts, independent study in the community, and a full complement of interscholastic sports.

Patricia R. Chadwick

Ada Byron Lovelace
First Computer Programmer

Ada Byron Lovelace was one of the most charming personalities in computer history. While she is known as a British mathematician and musician, Ada is best known as the first computer programmer. She wrote about Charles Babbage's "Analytical Engine", explaining the process with such clarity and precision that her work became the leading text explaining the process now known as computer programming. A software language that was developed in 1979 by the U.S. Department of Defense was named Ada in her honor.

Ada Byron Lovelace was born on December 10, 1815 to the famous poet, Lord Byron and Annabella Milbanke. Lord Byron was a strikingly handsome man who traveled widely and wrote his poetry with a biting criticism of British society. While he fell in love with Annabella, their marriage lasted only a year. Five weeks after Ada was born, Lady Bryon asked for a separation from her husband, and was given sole custody of the child. Lord Byron left for Italy and never returned to his home. He never saw his daughter again. He died in Greece when Ada was eight years old.

Ada was an active athletic child, loving gymnastics, dancing, and horseback riding. She became an accomplished musician, playing the piano, violin, and harp. As a teenager, Ada had all the advantages of the elite in London. She attended concerts, theaters, and elegant parties. She met many famous people, including the queen.

Even though she loved the arts, Ada was more interested in how things worked. She was fascinated by mechanical things and loved to figure out what made machines work. Lady Byron, being afraid that Ada would end up being a poet like her father, encouraged her daughter in her studies of mathematics and the sciences.

When she was seventeen years old, Ada met Mrs. Somerville, a remarkable woman who had just published a book on mathematical astronomy, "The Mechanism of the Heavens". This woman became a mentor to Ada and while she encouraged the young lady in her mathematical studies, she also tried to put mathematics and technology in a human context. It was Mrs. Somerville who arranged for Ada to meet Lord William King, Earl of Lovelace, who was to later become her husband.

Ada met Charles Babbage at a dinner party put on by Mrs. Somerville. It was here that she first heard of Mr. Babbage's Analytical Engine and Ada was intrigued by his ideas. As his idea progressed in later years, Ada suggested to Babbage that a plan be written for how the engine might calculate Bernoulli numbers. He commissioned Ada to write that plan, and this very plan is now considered the first "computer program".

After she wrote the description of Babbage's Analytical Engine, her life was difficult. She was plagued with illnesses and she died of cancer in 1852 at the age of 36.

Patricia R. Chadwick

Belva Lockwood
Pioneer Woman Lawyer

Belva A. Lockwood is one of America's most remarkable women, achieving marked success in the field of Law. In this profession, Belva was a pioneer in American and her career is the story of struggle and well-earned victories.

Belva Lockwood was born Belva A. Burnett in the town of Royalton, Niagara County, New York in 1830. When she was only fourteen she began teaching school. Though she earned only half the salary of a male teacher, she used her earnings to pay tuition to attend a local academy. Soon she married Mr. McNall, a local farmer. Together they had one daughter, but soon after the birth, Mr. McNall died, leaving Belva to support her family.

Belva returned to teaching but was also determined to continue her education. She entered Syracuse University (then called Genesee University) and graduated with honors in 1857. Upon graduation received an offer to become the principal of Lockport Union School. She accepted and remained employed there for four years. Afterwards she taught at Gainsville Seminary, and later founded the McNall Seminary at Oswego, N.Y.

In 1868 Belva moved to Washington, D.C. and opened a school there. It was there that she met Rev. Ezekiel Lockwood

and soon married him. It was around this time that Belva
began studying law and sought admission to the law school of
Columbia College. She was refused because of her sex, the
faculty feeling that her presence at the school would distract
the male students.

The following year Belva was admitted to the National
University Law School, from which she graduated. While this
was an accomplishment, Belva was unable to receive her
diploma until she appealed to the school's president, US
President Ulysses S. Grant. Finally, she received the degree of
B.L. from that school and opened a law practice in
Washington. Her clients consisted mainly of women, Native
Americans, and the poor. When one of Belva's cases reached
the Supreme Court, she was not legally able to argue the case
before it. While Belva was admitted to the bar of the District
of Columbia, she was refused admission to practice before the
Supreme Court. She spent the next five years lobbying for a
bill to pass through congress that would allow a woman to
practice law before the Supreme Court. In 1879, Belva
Lockwood had the honor of becoming the first woman
admitted to the Bar of the U.S. Supreme Court.

While Belva Lockwood is best known for her work in
opening up the legal profession to women, she was also a
staunch supporter of women's rights, working unceasingly to
secure the vote for women. She also was a strong advocate of
world peace and worked toward developing the rules for
international arbitration. She died a hero among women in
1917.

Patricia R. Chadwick

Antoinette Brown Blackwell
First Ordained Woman Minister in America

Antoinette Brown was born on May 20, 1825 to Joseph and Abby Brown, devout Christians, in the farming community of Henrietta, New York. Her parents valued education and sent all their children to local country schools at early ages. Netty, as she was fondly called, started attending school at the tender age of 3 years old.

As a young girl, Netty began to feel the call of God on her life to preach the Gospel. She was an unusually devout child and at the age of 9 was accepted as a member in her local Congregational Church that she attended with her family. She often spoke at meetings and testified of God's love and presence in her life. As she grew into a young woman, she longed to become a minister, but she cherished her dream in silence, since it was unheard of for a woman to be a pastor.

Netty spent three years continuing her education at Monroe Academy in Henrietta and began teaching in nearby country schools at the age of 15. She was an attractive young woman and had many suitors. Though she longed for a husband and a family of her own, God's call on her life to become a minister kept her from marriage. Against her parent's wishes, she made plans to attend Oberlin Collegiate

55

Institute in Ohio, a relatively new school that admitted women. She also chose this school because of the theological school attached to it. She worked for 3 years to earn her tuition and at 21 years of age she set off for Oberlin College.

After completing two years in the Ladies Literary Course with an excellent academic record, Netty applied for admission the theological school. She was met with disbelief and anger. While Oberlin admitted women students to its institution, much of the faculty still did not support coeducation and women were not allowed to study theology. But while most of the professors objected to her being admitted into the theological school, Oberlin's charter stated that the college facilities must be open to everyone, regardless of race, color, or sex. Though they didn't want to admit her, the faculty could find no grounds for refusing her. Finally, she was permitted to attend classes in the theological school, but she was not accepted as a registered student.

Netty completed the course in theology in the allotted 2 years, earning her the money for tuition and board by housekeeping and teaching an art class. During the time in the theological school, she completed a 30 page exegesis demonstrating that St. Paul's words that seemed to limit a woman's role in the church were being misinterpreted. This research project was to be used by countless women in the future as they struggled for equal rights. As graduation drew near, Antoinette applied with the men students to the trustees for a license to preach. She was refused under the pretense that since she was not a registered student, they could not give her the license. Neither was she allowed to participate in graduation exercises.

Discouraged, Netty returned home. There her family pleaded with her to give up the idea of becoming a minister, but Netty could not comply. While home, she was contacted by Lucy Stone, a fellow student from Oberlin, to come and speak at a woman's rights convention in Massachusetts regarding the status of women as set forth in Scripture. This first speaking engagement took Netty one step closer to the realization of her dream.

She became a lecturer of reform for the abolition of slavery, temperance, and woman's rights. A wealthy woman reformer paid for Netty's expenses and though she was not a pastor, she felt she was doing the Lord's work. To her delight, after many lectures, she was often asked to stay over and preach.

Antoinette receive much exposure on the lecture circuit and in 1853 she was finally offered a position as pastor of a small Congregational Church in South Butler, New York. She was ordained to the ministry by the Reverend Luther Lee, a prominent Congregationalist from Syracuse, thus becoming the first regularly ordained woman of a recognized denomination.

Later in life, Netty resigned her pulpit in South Butler and married Samuel Blackwell, brother of Elizabeth Blackwell, the first woman in America to receive a degree in medicine. She found great happiness and fulfillment as a wife and mother of six daughters. While she always took care of her family's needs first, she continued to preach and lecture as time permitted. She also took up writing and published nine more books and hundreds of articles.

Antoinette Brown Blackwell became one of the most revered women of America and countless people were moved by her gospel of love. Throughout her life she was at the forefront of reform movements of all kinds and a pioneer in the woman's rights movement. Her strength and perseverance in pursuing her goal of becoming a minister helped pave the way for other women to seek fulfillment of their own dreams, never before thought possible.

Patricia R. Chadwick

Elizabeth Blackwell
First Woman to Receive an M.D. Degree

While many nineteenth century doctors, including some women, practiced medicine without a degree, Elizabeth Blackwell was the first to attain full professional status. She is the first woman in America to obtain an M.D. degree.

Though she was born in England, Elizabeth's parents moved the family to America when she was only ten years old. Her father failed in business in New York and a few years later died, leaving a wife and nine children nearly penniless. For seven years, she, with two sisters, taught at a young ladies' seminary and nearly supported the entire family.

When she was about twenty-two years old, Elizabeth determined to study medicine along with her teaching. After a few years of study by herself, she moved to Charleston, South Carolina, where she taught music and studied medicine under Dr. Samuel H. Dickson. Later she moved to Philadelphia to study under Dr. J.M. Allen.

Though she applied to the medical schools of Philadelphia, New York, and Boston, she was refused admission because of her sex. The schools used the excuse that there was no precedent and that it was improper to break away from established custom. She did not give up, however, and was finally admitted to the college at Geneva, N.Y. and pursued her studies with marked success and took her degree in 1849. Her repeated declaration was "There is some place in the world for me and I'll find it." (King, *Woman*, p. 440).

She pursued clinical studies in Blockley hospital in Philadelphia and then went to Paris to study in the Maternite Hospital. Her next experience was in the hospital of St. Bartholomew in London, where she spent a year. She then returned to New York where she wished to set up a medical practice.

This was easier said than done. She could find no place to hang her sign. Hospitals and dispensaries refused association with her and she was even refused lodging and office space. While these things were sometimes hard to bear, instead of discouraging her, difficulties made Elizabeth more determined. She began to see women and children in her home and as her practice developed she also wrote lectures on health, which she published in 1852 under the title *The Laws of Life: with Special Reference to the Physical Education of Girls.*

About the time Elizabeth established her practice in New York, her sister Emily Blackwell began to study medicine also. She graduated from the Cleveland College in 1854, having also studied in the Rush Medical College in Chicago. She spent a year in Edinburgh, Paris, and London. Upon her return to America, she became a close associate of her sister, Elizabeth, in New York. Through their efforts the "New York

Infirmary for Women and Children" was established. The object was first, a charity for the poor, second, a resort for respectable patients desiring special treatment, and third, a place to which female students might come for practical clinical study.

Elizabeth Blackwell was an inspiration to women all over the world to strive to achieve their dreams. She at last won the victory and prepared the way for others to win success and honor.

Lucy Webb Hayes
First Temperance First Lady

Lucy Webb Hayes was the wife of U.S. President Rutherford B. Hayes. In her 37 years of marriage to Mr. Hayes, Lucy developed a keen understanding of politics. Yet it was due to her intelligence, acts of kindness, temperance work, and charitable deeds, that she remained a legend in Washington long after she left the White House.

Lucy Webb Hayes was born in 1831 the daughter of Dr, James Webb and Maria Cook Hayes in Ohio. Lucy lost her father, however, at the age of two. When she was just entering her teens, the family moved to the town of Delaware so that her two brothers could enroll in the Ohio Wesleyan University. Lucy, herself, a devout Christian, was educated at the Wesleyan Female College in Cincinnati where she graduated from at the age of eighteen.

In 1852 she married Rutherford B. Hayes and lived in Cincinnati until the Civil War began. Rutherford soon began to share his wife's deeply religious opposition to slavery and he soon joined the Union army along with her brothers. Lucy gave much time to nursing sick and wounded soldiers, both in her home and on the front lines. She was affectionately known as "Mother Lucy" to the men of the 23rd Ohio

Volunteer Infantry who served under her husband's command in the war. She spent two winters in camp and served in the hospital at Frederick City, Maryland.

Lucy was an untiring worker in humanitarian and religious causes and while her husband was a member of Congress and then Governor of Ohio, she devoted much time and talent to state charities, such as helping organize the Ohio Soldiers' and Sailors' Orphans' Home.

In 1877 Rutherford Benjamin Hayes took up the duties of President of the United States and Lucy entered her position as First Lady with confidence gained from her long and happy married life, her vast knowledge of politics, and her cheerful spirit. She enjoyed her position as First Lady and instituted many changes.

Lucy was a woman of conviction who was a firm believer in temperance. She determined that the White House should be a religious and temperance house so long as she remained in it. She stood firm in her convictions and did not serve liquor or wine at the White House, even at State Dinners. This was an unexpected change for Washington society, but Mrs. Hayes would not go against her conscience because of the derision of the Washington elite. Lucy often received criticism for her stance on alcohol, yet she still became one of the best-loved First Ladies. She often used her position as First Lady to bring pleasure to others.

Lucy Webb Hayes died on June 25, 1889. At her death

flags were lowered to half-mast in many American communities in honor of the first lady who was considered the most "amiable, sincere, and most idolized woman in America" (King, *Woman*, p.499).

Patricia R. Chadwick

Francis Folsom Cleveland
First White House Bride

Frances Folsom Cleveland holds the distinction of being the
first bride of a President to be married in the White House.
She was only twenty-two years old when she took over the
duties of First Lady under the administration of her new
husband, Grover Cleveland.

Frances was born Frances Folsom in 1864 to Oscar Folsom
and Emma C. Harmon Folsom in Buffalo, New York. Her
father was a lawyer and became a law partner of Grover
Cleveland's before his death when Frances was only eleven
years old. Upon the death of her husband, Emma moved with
her daughter to Medina, New York, where they stayed for
only a few years. Upon their return to Buffalo, Frances
entered the Central High School, where she prepared for
college. Grover Cleveland stayed a close friend of the family.
As administrator of the Folsom estate after Oscar's death, he
guided Frances' education with sound advice. Frances was
extremely bright and so thorough in her studies that she was
allowed to enter college as a sophomore at Wells College.

When Frances entered Wells College, Mr. Cleveland asked
permission from Mrs. Folsom to correspond with her
daughter. At the time of her graduation from college in 1885,

Frances received a superb floral tribute from the White House conservatories. The affection they had for each other turned into romance, despite their 27-year difference in age. After graduation, Frances went abroad with her mother, but returned the following spring. Though no public announcement had been made of her engagement to Grover Cleveland, the interested public was sure there would be one. Upon landing in New York, Frances was met by Grover's sister, Rose Elizabeth Cleveland and his private secretary. The wedding took place on June 2, 1886 in the blue room of the White House.

The first fifteen months of his first term as president, Grover's sister Rose played hostess. She gladly gave up these duties to Frances and the new First Lady occupied the position with rare grace. For one so young it was an exhausting position, but at no time did she ever forget the dignity of her position. Mrs. Cleveland's charm and grace won her immediate popularity. She was very thoughtful and held two receptions every week, one on Saturday afternoons, when women with jobs were free to come.

After the President lost the next election, the couple resided in New York City. It was there they had a daughter, Ruth. In 1893, Grover Cleveland was re-elected President and he and Frances returned to the White House. The First Lady was welcomed with most cordial affection as if she'd only been gone a day instead of four years.

The Clevelands had two more children along while holding office as President at First Lady. Esther was born in

1893 in the White House; Marion was born in 1895 at their summer home, Gray Gables. When the family left the White House, Mrs. Cleveland had become one of the most popular First Ladies to ever serve in the White House.

Frances bore two sons while the Clevelands lived in Princeton, New Jersey. She was with her husband when he died at their home, "Westland", in 1908. Still being a fairly young woman, Frances was married again in 1913, to Thomas J. Preston, Jr., a professor of archeology at Princeton. She died in 1947 at the age of 84. Up until the time of her death she was noted for her charitable work and charming personality. But she was most admired for her devotion to her children.

Baroness Burdett-Coutts
First Woman to Receive the Title of Baroness for Her Good Works

British philanthropist, Baroness Angela Georgina Burdett-Coutts, used much of her inherited wealth to promote charitable works in her nation and abroad. She gave financial support to schools, churches, and housing development throughout Great Britain and gave aid to those overseas.

Angela was born to Sir Francis Burdett, Baronet, but her great wealth came from her grandfather, Thomas Coutts, the noted banker. She joined the name of both her father and grandfather and became known as Angela Gerogina Burdett-Coutts. In 1881 she married William Lehman Ashmead Bartlett, who by royal license took the name of Burdett-Coutts.

The baroness had always been a remarkable administrator. She possessed discernment and upon finding out the needs of individuals or groups, she took the initiative to improve their conditions. One of her first great works was to establish a home for young women who had turned aside from a path of virtue. Nearly half of those who came to the home permanently left their life of vice.

Spitalfields in London was a section of destitution. To

help improve the situation for those living there, the baroness established a sewing school for women where they could be taught, fed, and provided with work. From this place nurses were sent out to the sick of that community. In 1859, several hundred impoverished boys were fitted out for the Royal Navy or placed in industrial homes.

Another immoral, disease-ridden spot in London was Nova Scotia Gardens. Angela purchased this section and upon what was a literal dumping ground of the city she erected model dwellings for about two hundred families, to be rented out at a moderate price.

When the cry came from suffering humanity in Ireland, Scotland, Turkey, and different parts of the world, Baroness Burdett-Coutts was among the first to respond. For needy fishermen she provided both temporary and permanent relief by furnishing them with food, clothing, tackle, and boats. In Australia she founded an organization to aid the aborigines and she began a relief fund for refugees of the 1877 Russo-Turkish War.

Baroness Angelina Georgina Burdett-Coutts was certainly a princess of philanthropy and charity. In 1871 she became the first woman to be honored with a baronage for public achievement. She died in 1906 and is buried in Westminster Abbey.

Amelia Earhart
First Woman to Fly Solo Across the Atlantic

Amelia Earhart was born July 24, 1898 in Atchison, Kansas. She was a lively tomboy throughout her childhood and unlike most American women in her generation and generations before, she never outgrew this trait. She volunteered in a Red Cross Hospital during World War I, taught English to immigrant factory workers, and studied pre-med for a short time. But airplanes were her first love.

Amelia loved excitement. Impressed with stunt fliers and air shows, Amelia learned to fly and became a licensed pilot, making her first solo flight in 1921. Soon she saved enough money to buy her own plane.

In 1928, Amelia was asked to be a part of a team of pilots that was to make a transatlantic flight. She accepted and became the first woman to fly across the Atlantic Ocean. She was hallowed by the press and dubbed "Lady Lindy", winning public affection. But Amelia was not satisfied with this. Because of her adventurous spirit and love for the spotlight, Amelia became determined to perfect her flying skills, making plans to fly the ocean on her own. This she did on May 20, 1932.

Amelia achieved a number of flight "firsts". She was the first woman pilot to fly the Pacific Ocean and the first woman to make a transcontinental flight in an autogyro, the predecessor of the helicopter, which was still in its developmental stage. But while attempting to fly around the world in 1937, Amelia's plane vanished and she was presumed lost at sea. She was 39 years old.

Amelia Earhart was a woman of great courage. She chose to loose herself from the conventional roles of women in her generation and follow her heart, doing what she loved best - flying.

3

Social Reformers

Harriet Beecher Stowe
The Little Woman Who Started the Big War

Julia Ward Howe
Author of the Battle Hymn of the Republic

Dorothea Dix
Advocate for the Imprisoned & the Mentally Ill

Helen Hunt Jackson
Champion of the American Indians

Anna Dickinson
Abolitionist

Grimke Sisters
Southern Abolitionists

Francis Willard
Temperance Leader

Lady Henry Somerset
British Temperance Leader

Anna Jarvis
Founder of Mother's Day

Clara Barton
Angel of the Battlefield

Helen Miller Gould
Philanthropist

Francis Powers Cobb
Founder of Ragged Schools

Harriet Beecher Stowe
The Little Woman Who Started the Big War

When President Abraham Lincoln met Harriet Beecher Stowe in 1862, he exclaimed, "So you are the little woman who wrote the book that started this Great War!" He was referring to her book, *Uncle Tom's Cabin* where Harriet expressed her moral outrage at the institution of slavery in the United States and exposed its harmful effects on both whites and blacks.

Harriet Beecher Stowe was born in Litchfield, Connecticut on June 14, 1811 in into one of America's most notable religious families. The Beecher family was at the forefront of numerous reform movements of the 19th century. Born the seventh child of the well-known Congregational minister Lyman Beecher and Roxana Foote Beecher, she was their fourth daughter. Her father was a persuasive preacher, theologian, and founder of the American Bible Society, who also was active in the anti-slavery movement. Her mother was a woman of prayer, who asked the Lord to put the call of service on her children's hearts. This prayer was eventually answered in a mighty way. All the Beecher children spent their lives living out their Christian faith.

While Harriet's life was not without trials, she appears to have had a relatively good family life. When she was only four years old, her mother died, leaving her father to become the dominant adult influence upon the home. While it must have been difficult to both support the family financially as well emotionally, it appears he did a fine job raising his family. According to Harriet, he made the home a kind of "moral heaven", discussing theology over family apple peelings and always keeping before them the haloed memory of their dear mother. Her father did remarry a few years after her mother's death, but Roxana's children never quite took to their stepmother and continued to cling to their father for love and spiritual guidance. While Lyman struggled with mood swings and often felt like he couldn't go on, the sincere way he lived his life inspired in all his children a quiet ambition for some large service. And Harriet was no exception.

Harriet was given a good education. At eight she began to attend the famed school of Miss Sarah Peirce in Litchfield, where she studied until she was thirteen when she left home to attend the female seminary recently opened by her sister Catharine in Hartford. Harriet was quite shy and kept to herself, but she loved to read and write. Among her favorite books were Scott's "Ballads" and "Arabian Nights", which no doubt had much to do with cultivating her imagination.

While home during the summer leave when she was thirteen years old, Harriet gave her life to Christ during one of her father's sermons and felt the assurance of Christ's saving love. Within the Beecher family, private conversion was intertwined with a public calling, and this decision to follow Christ would shape the rest of Harriet's life.

At the age of fifteen she became an assistant to her sister Catharine in the female seminary and continued teaching there until 1832 when the family moved to Cincinnati, Ohio where

75

Lyman felt called to "win the West for God". Lyman became President of Lane Theological Seminary and Pastor of the Second Presbyterian Church and Catharine founded the Western Female Institute. Harriet taught in Catherine's school and wrote a children's geography text, which was her first publication, though the first edition was issued under her sister's name.

It was here that, Harriet met Calvin Stowe, a professor and clergyman fervently opposed to slavery. In 1836, at the age of 25, Harriet married Professor Stowe, a widower, who was nine years her senior. They were to have seven children together and Harriet proved to be a fine homemaker as she lovingly cared for her children, which was her main priority. She saw motherhood as sacredly sacrificial and set out to follow her calling of raising children that loved and served God. But Calvin's teaching position did not provide a sufficient wage, so in order to supplement Calvin's meager teaching salary, Harriet wrote short stories dealing with domestic life for local and religious magazines and papers. Her royalties helped her hire household staff to assist with the running of the household and raising her children.

Calvin and Harriet were blessed with a loving marriage. Both encouraged and comforted each other during the trials and tribulations that came their way. During their lifetime they lost four of their seven children and had many financial setbacks. While they did not have a perfect marriage, their loving commitment grew solidly over the years. At one point Harriet wrote to her husband of many years, "If you were not already my dearly beloved husband, I should certainly fall in love with you." Calvin encouraged Harriet to establish a

Patricia R. Chadwick

writing career, and he served as her literary agent in both America and England. She in turn encouraged him to write himself and he, too, met with some success.

While they lived in Ohio, the work of the Underground Railroad deeply touched both Calvin and Harriet. Their house was one of the many "stations" for the fugitive slaves on their way to freedom in Canada. They sheltered runaway slaves in their home until they move to Maine when Calvin accepted a position at Bowdoin College in 1850.

Throughout America's history, the slavery issue has been hotly debated. By the late 1840's the abolitionist movement had expanded, roused by newspaper editors, lecturers, authors, and clergymen. For abolitionists, nothing justified slavery. It was in this environment that Mrs. Stowe wrote her famous novel *Uncle Tom's Cabin*. In this book, Harriet dispelled the myth that benevolent masters treated their slaves adequately. She showed that even kind-hearted slave owners would separate slave families and sell them "down the river" when they were desperate for cash. Harriet drew on her own personal experience with slavery in writing her book. She was familiar slavery, the anti-slavery movement, and the Underground Railroad because she spent many years living in Ohio, and Kentucky, a neighboring state across the Ohio River from Cincinnati, Ohio, was a slave state.

It was soon after the passage of the Fugitive Slave Act of 1850 that Harriet wrote *Uncle Tom's Cabin*. The Fugitive Slave Act granted Southerners the right to pursue fugitive slaves into free states and bring them back. This law aroused may abolitionists to action. When the South threatened to secede, Harriet determined that she would write a serial

77

condemning the evils of slavery. First printed as a serial in an abolitionist paper, *The National Era*, it focused public interest on the issue of slavery, and was deeply controversial. In 1852 *Uncle Tom's Cabin* was printed in book form. It sold 3,000 copies on its first day, 300,000 its first year, and eventually sold more than 3,000,000 copies worldwide (James, *Notable Women*, p. 397).

Uncle Tom's Cabin was the first major American novel to feature a black hero. Harriet created memorable characters that portrayed the inhumanity of slavery making her readers understand that slaves were people who were being mistreated and made to suffer at the hands of their masters. Through her novel, Harriet insisted that slavery eroded the moral sensibility of whites that tolerated or profited from it. She wrote passionately to prick the consciences of fellow Americans to end their blind allegiance to slavery.

Many people of her day argued that her novel was merely fiction and not at all based on fact. To disprove these accusations and prove that her depiction of slavery was factual, in 1853, Harriet wrote *A Key to Uncle Tom's Cabin*, which presented the original facts and documents upon which she based her novel.

The historical significance of Harriet's abolitionists writing has veiled from view her other work and literary significance. Her writings were varied and in many different genre. She wrote both fiction and biography along with children's books. Some feel that her best works are about New England life such as *The Ministers Wooing* and *Old Town Folks*, where her settings were accurately described in detail. Her portraits of local social life, particularly of minor characters, reflect and

78

ability to communicate to others the culture in which she lived.

Julia Ward Howe
Author of the Battle Hymn of the Republic

While she was active in many social reform movements of her day, Julia Ward Howe is perhaps best known as being the author of one of the great rallying songs of the Civil War Era, *The Battle Hymn of the Republic*. The words for this hymn first appeared in the February 1862, issue of *The Atlantic Monthly* magazine and were considered by many as the Civil War's battle song of the Republic.

Julia Ward Howe was born on May 27, 1819 into a prominent New York City family that had a distinguished lineage on both sides. Though she was raised in a conservative, Christian home, she rebelled against the strict religious views of her father, becoming a liberal thinker. Yet Julia maintained a firm belief in a personal, loving God and a strong faith in Christ.

Since her mother died when she was only five years old, She was raised by her father with the help of various members of her extended family. Her father saw to it that she received the best education available, attending various private girls' schools also being tutored at home. She grew into a gracious and intelligent young woman with a strong literary bent. Due to her marked abilities, she was readily accepted into the society of such notables as Margaret Fuller, Horace Mann, and Ralph Waldo Emerson.

In 1843, Julia married the Boston Reformer, Dr. Samuel G. Howe, nearly 20 years her senior. It proved to be a rather stormy marriage. Even though Dr. Howe was involved in numerous reform movements, he was strongly opposed to married women being involved in public life. While he permitted his wife to assist him "behind the scenes" in his own work, for years she was limited in her work and her role was largely that of an impatient onlooker, especially as the troubled events of the 1850's led her husband to become an active abolitionist.

She did, however, pursue her writing career, even against her husband's wishes. In 1854, despite her husband's disapproval, Julia anonymously published her first volume of poems, *Passions Flowers*. It was met with success and she continued writing and publishing volumes of poetry, several plays, and many magazine articles on various themes. This caused friction between husband and wife as Dr. Howe emphatically objected to Julia's speaking in public and her literary career.

In the fall of 1861, after the Civil War began, Mrs. Howe accompanied her husband to Washington, D.C., where he was involved in medical service for the government. During the visit, Julia became deeply disturbed as she noted the growing angry mood of the Nation. Mrs. Howe daily watched troops marching off to war singing *John Brown's Body,* a song about an unconventional man who had been hanged in his efforts to free the slaves. One day, a friend suggested that she write some "decent words for that tune". Julia agreed. That evening, after retiring to bed, the words came to Julia. She rose in the predawn hours and scrawled the verses of the poem that was

to become famous as ***The Battle Hymn of the Republic***
(James, *Notable Women,* p. 227). The poem was published in
the ***Atlantic Monthly*** and Mrs. Howe received a mere $5 for
this literary work. But soon regiments all over the north were
singing the song and it wasn't long before the entire nation
was united in singing, "Mine eyes have seen the glory of the
coming of the Lord..." It is recorded that this hymn was sung
as a solo at a large patriotic rally that was attended by
President Abraham Lincoln. It is said that after the audience
had responded with loud applause, the President, with tears in
his eyes, shouted, "Sing it again!" And it was sung again and
again for well over a hundred years, becoming one of our
finest national hymns, finding its way into almost every
American hymnal.

In the postwar years, her husband finally gave up his
violent opposition to Julia's public life and she became a
leader in her own right. Mrs. Howe became involved in the
Woman's Suffrage Movement, joining with Lucy Stone to
form the American Woman Suffrage Association and began
actively promoting a suffrage amendment. She became a
frequent lecturer at conventions and legislative hearings and
was founder, editor, and contributor to a weekly publication
called ***Woman's Journal.*** She not only fought for a woman's
right to vote, but also struggled to free women from traditional
stereotypes, especially in marriage, that kept women from
sharing their ideas or becoming all that God intended them to
be.

By the time she reached her eighties, Julia had become a
national figure, beloved by the American people. In 1908, two
years before she died at the age of ninety-one, Julia Ward

Howe was the first woman to be elected to the prestigious American Academy of Arts and Letters.

Dorothea Dix
Advocate for the Imprisoned & the Mentally Ill

One of the most wonderful women of the nineteenth century was Dorothea L. Dix. Though she was a frail and overworked woman, she had a gentle, loving disposition, but with a will like steel. She worked hard against apathy and other fearful odds while working for the betterment of the imprisoned and mentally ill, and she never once failed.

Dorothea was born at Hampden, Maine the daughter of Mary Bigelow and Joseph Dix. Her father was a Methodist preacher. Her family passed down a strong social conscious to the young girl along with an interest in healing and philanthropy.

Born into a family of modest means, she helped support her family by running a school for young children in Boston when she was nineteen years old. Over the next few years published several children's books. Illness forced her to close the school, and in an attempt to restore her health she went on a lengthy trip to England. There she came to know many English reformers, and began to take an active part in humanitarian causes.

By the late 1830's, Boston, where she now lived, was full of humanitarian people. Dorothea was among those who wanted to better society. In 1841, hearing that a Sunday-school teacher was needed in the East Cambridge House of Correction, she volunteered to teach a class of twenty women who were criminals and drunkards.

When she visited the jail she found some mentally ill people confined in unheated rooms. In order to correct the abuse she witnessed, Dorothea had to bring the matter into court. Armed with a shocking array of facts, she petitioned the legislature "in behalf of the insane paupers confined within the Commonwealth in cages, closets, cellars, stalls, pens; chained, naked, beaten with rods and lashed into obedience." (James, *Notable Women*, 487). Because of her efforts, these abuses were largely corrected in Massachusetts, encouraging her to undertake reform in other states. New Jersey was her next field, where, by careful investigation and wise presentation, she won victories for the insane and criminals.

It is amazing that in less than four years' work she visited and investigated eighteen states prisons, three hundred county jails and houses of correction, and more than five hundred almshouses. Everywhere she met sights, which were sickening and horrible, but though weak in body and at times sick, she bravely toiled on.

Dorothea's reform work extended past the borders of her own nation. Miss Dix visited Halifax and Toronto, brought reform to Scotland, and visited hospitals in Norway, Holland, Italy, Russia, and Greece. She awakened the slumbering moral sense of the people and the treatment of the inmates of asylums and prisons was revolutionized.

At the outbreak of the Civil War in America, she gave herself to the work of nursing in the army and was made chief of army nurses. What Florence Nightingale was to the Crimean War, the same was Dorothea Dix to the Union Army during the Civil War. She was sixty-three years old and weighed only ninety-five pounds when the war was over. She remained in Washington during the heat of the summer to visit hospitals and carry on a vast correspondence in her attempt to locate missing sons, fathers, husbands, and sweethearts. She worked at this until the last weeks of 1866.

For the next fifteen years she traveled the country working in the behalf of the mentally ill. Many of the institutions she had helped to establish suffered neglect during the war, prompting her to say: "It would seem all my work is to be done over. (King, *Woman,* p. 372).

For the last fifty years of her life, Dorothea had no home and often lived in the quarters of the hospitals she founded. In 1882 she became quite ill and after five years of suffering she died at Trenton Asylum, which was offered to her as a retreat and she lovingly called it her "firstborn child". She was buried in Mount Auburn Cemetery near Boston.

The life of Dorothea Lynde Dix was one of great love and sacrifice on behalf of mankind. Her life was an expression of the Christian way of life at its very best.

Patricia R. Chadwick

Helen Hunt Jackson
Champion of the American Indian

Helen Hunt Jackson was born on October 18, 1931 as Helen
Maria Fiske.   She was born and raised in Amherst,
Massachusetts.   Helen Maria Fiske.   Helen grew up in a
literary atmosphere and she was herself a poet and writer of
children's stories, novels, and essays. She published her work
under the pen name of H.H.H. Her poetry was the outflow of
deep sympathetic thought on the problem of life's trials and
temptations. Her verses were strong and noble, never giving
attention to mere prettiness of verse. One of her early works,
"Bits of Travel", revealed the humorous side of her nature.
With friendly merriment she describes human nature (King,
Woman, p. 404).

Soon, Helen's interests turned to the plight of the
American Indian. As a keen and sympathetic observer, her
attention was attracted by the unfair treatment our American
Indians received at the hands of government agents.   Her
interest in the American Indians began in Boston in 1879 at a
lecture by Chief Standing Bear, who described the ill
treatment of the Ponca Indians in Nebraska.   Helen was
furious by what she heard, but being well balanced by nature,
she made a painstaking study of the situation. She kept her
feelings in check and searched for facts. When she was at last
fully equipped for her work, she took up the pen in defense of

the wronged Indian. Due to her poor health, Helen wrote with desperate haste. *A Century of Dishonor* appeared calling for change from the vile, selfish policy to a treatment characterized by humanity and justice.

Her next step was to cast her material in the form of fiction to reach a wider circle of readers. She wrote **Ramona**, which was her supreme effort. It was in every way a noble book and gave Helen lasting fame. **Ramona** first appeared as a serial in the *Christian Union*, because she was anxious to get the story out.

Helen died in San Francisco on August 12, 1885, while she was examining the condition of the California Indians as a special government commissioner.

Patricia R. Chadwick

Anna Dickinson
Abolitionist

Anna E. Dickinson was born in 1842 to John and Mary Dickinson. Her father was a Philadelphia merchant and her mother was from an aristocratic family and very refined. Both were devout Quakers and of noble character. When Anna was an infant, the family lost their property and was reduced to poverty. Furthermore, the family suffered a greater loss when her father, who was a staunch abolitionist, died from a heart attack after giving an agitating anti-slavery speech in 1844, when Anna was only two years old.

Anna grew into a restless, willful, yet imaginative child, who cause her family much anxiety. Her childhood was not an easy one. Her more wealthy schoolmates made fun of her poor clothes and this caused her to strive to better herself. She read everything within her reach. Anna's ambition and stubbornness were traits that fueled her determination. She had a passion for rhetoric and on one occasion scrubbed sidewalks for twenty-five cents so she could hear Wendell Phillips lecture on "The Lost Arts".

In 1860, Anna made her first speech on "Woman's Rights and Wrongs" before the Association of Progressive Friends. After this she turned to the lecture circuit and made lecturing her profession.   She spoke on such topics as abolition, woman's rights, and wartime issues. One of her most notable lectures, delivered after the close of the war, was *Woman's Work and Wages*, a topic on which she spoke with great passion (Patron, *Eminent Women,* p. 496).

Probably the greatest honor of her life was an invitation to speak in the Hall of Representatives. Assembled to hear her were one of the most notable audiences that ever met in Washington.   Many senators, representatives, foreign diplomats, the chief justice, the president, and much of Washington society in general came out to hear her. The proceeds of this lecture were over one thousand dollars and were devoted to the National Freedmen's Relief Society.

Although Anna Dickinson worked unceasingly for social reform during her lifetime, before her death in 1932, her impact on abolition, the woman's rights movement, and the North's success in the Civil War were all but forgotten.

Patricia R. Chadwick

Grimké Sister's
Southern Abolitionists

Sarah and Angelina Grimké were American feminists and social reformers that spent their lives working and leading in both the abolitionist and suffrage movements. Because they were refined, wealthy southern women, their speeches and writings against slavery attracted considerable attention.

Sarah and Angelina Grimké (pronounced GRIHM kee) were born in Charleston, South Carolina in 1792 and 1805 respectively. They were the daughters of John F. Grimké and Mary Smith Grimké. Their father was a slave-holding judge and their mother came from a family prominent in South Carolina politics. Sarah was the sixth of fourteen children and Angelina was the last. Among their siblings were Thomas Smith Grimké, a lawyer, state senator, and advocate of peace, temperance, and educational reforms and Frederick Grimké who became a judge of the Ohio Supreme Court.

The Grimké sisters received an education that was considered suitable for young ladies of their day. Private tutors in the "proper" subjects educated them, but Sarah protested when she was denied being taught Greek, Latin, philosophy and law. Since she was not allowed formal education in these areas, she learned all she could from her

91

father and brothers.

In 1821, Sarah left Charleston because of her strong antislavery views and moved to Philadelphia. She had come to know many Quakers, whom she admired because of their simplicity, sincerity, and piety and she joined herself to that group once moving to Philadelphia. Angelina joined her in Philadelphia in 1829 and together they set out to end the evil of slavery in our nation.

Both sisters gave antislavery lectures in several Northeastern states and were some of the first women to lecture in public in the United States. Angelina appealed to the women of America to support their fight against slavery in her works *Appeal to the Christian Women of the South*, published in1836 and *Appeal to Women of the Nominally Free States*, published in 1837. Sarah, too, began to write to gain support for abolition and in 1836 she published *Epistle to the Clergy of the Southern States*. Because of these and other writings, both Sarah and Angelina were threatened with imprisonment if they were ever to return to South Carolina. Regardless, they freed their family's slaves that were left to them as part of their father's estate.

Sarah and Angelina moved to New York in 1836 and became the first women to lecture for the American Anti-slavery Society. These appearances before mixed audiences soon thrust the Grimké sisters into the center of a controversy of the rights of women, one of the first in American history Lumpkin, *Emancipation,* p. 132). They were derided by much of the established clergy for their "unwomanly behavior" and this controversy actually broadened concern to include women's emancipation. It is both Sarah and Angelina who are credited for linking the anti-slavery and women's rights movements. The Grimké sister's argued that the fight for women's rights and the fight for abolition both supported human rights, but other abolitionists considered women's rights an unrelated issue.

Angelina married fellow abolitionist Theodore Weld in 1838, but Sarah remained single. Both sisters continued to lecture and teach until they both retired from public life in 1867, Sarah joining the Welds. Both sisters continued to work occasionally for both the abolitionist and women's rights movements. Sarah died in 1873 at eighty-one years old. Her death was officially attributed to laryngitis. Shortly after Angelina suffered a stroke and lived in this partially invalid state for six years, dying in 1879.

Francis Willard
Temperance Leader

Frances Elizabeth Willard was born on September 28, 1839 in Churchville, New York to Josiah Flint Willard and Mrs. Mary Thompson Hill Willard. Frances' early girlhood was spent on a farm on the frontier in what was then the territory of Wisconsin. Her parents were both teachers who made sure their children were well educated.

At seventeen, Frances and her sister Mary went to Milwaukee Female College, where their mother's sister, Sarah Hill, was teacher. From there she went on to Northwest Female College at Evanston, Illinois, where she graduated with high honors. In fact, she was valedictorian of her class.

After graduation, Frances taught continuously until 1868 when she went on a world tour with her friend Kate Jackson. Upon returning to America in 1870, Frances returned to Evanston and became President of Norwest Female College. Her teaching career lasted sixteen years. She taught in schools, seminaries, and colleges, her last position being that of Dean of the Woman's College of the Northwestern University. She was at the same time professor of aesthetics and natural science. One of Frances' great achievements was the introduction of the system of self-government among the students and bringing to pass its successful operation (King,

Woman, p. 413).

The next period of her life is marked by the temperance crusade in Ohio. Frances' soul was deeply stirred and she joined the temperance movement. The making of the Woman's College an extension of the University prevented her from carrying out her plans for the college, so she resigned her position as dean and professor and joined the temperance crusade movement.

From teaching aesthetics in a university she became an apostle of temperance to the drunkards in Chicago. Frances gave up much for temperance work. She often went without her lunch because she had no money to pay for it, and she walked several miles because she was unable to pay carfare.

Frances had a great administrative ability and she had a magnificent power over her audiences. The work grew and the combination of her abilities led her to become leader of the National and then the World's Woman's Christian Temperance Union.

Frances Willard was the most influential leader in the Temperance Movement in the United States. She was the originator of the motto: "For God, Home, and Native Land". In January 1898, Frances gave her last public address in the Congregational Church of Janesville.

Francis Willard died in February of 1898 due to contracting a rare form of anemia. Thousands of people from all over the world paid tribute to this wonderful woman at her funeral in New York City. As the train was carrying her body back to Chicago for burial, it made a brief stop in her hometown of Churchville, New York. Again, thousands of mourners passed in front of her casket, paying their respects. After her death, the state of Illinois donated a figure of Francis to the U.S. Capitol's Statuary Hall, the only woman to receive that honor (Janney, *Great Women,* p.292).

Patricia R. Chadwick

Lady Henry Somerset
British Temperance Leader

Lady Henry Somerset was born as Isabel Cocks in 1851, the first child of John Somers Cocks, third Earl of Somers. Her father was a nobleman in every way. For some years he was Lord-in-waiting to the Queen, spending the time at Windsor, Osborne, and Balmoral. Being a man of artistic and literary tastes, he resigned his position to devote himself to his studies, yet his intimate acquaintance with the Queen gave his daughter many advantages.

As a young woman Isabel was very beautiful. She was presented at court at nineteen and married at the age of twenty-two to Lord Henry Somerset, second son of the Duke of Beaufort. The marriage was arranged and while Isabel was an heiress to estates, manor houses, and London property, Somerset, as the second son, was penniless. The marriage was not a success and Isabel became a very independent woman. Soon she separated from her husband, who allegedly abused her. She left the Church of England and attached herself to the Methodists.

Lady Somerset owned a vast estate at Eastnor, fifteen miles in length, containing twenty-five thousand acres. Her house, which was a castle, was three miles from the lodge gate in Eastnor Park. In London she owned property where one hundred and twenty-five thousand people lived. She devoted much of her time and income to the welfare of the people of England. She began by studying the causes of poverty and crime, and found the liquor traffic at the bottom of it all. Being a woman of deeds as well as words, she took the total abstinence pledge, induced some of her tenants to do the same, and so started a temperance society. She visited the homes of her tenants, gave Bible readings in the kitchens, and gathered the mothers at her castle to discuss with them the training of their children.

Her philanthropic work soon spread beyond her own estates and call came for her to speak and work in behalf of temperance far and near. She went among the miners of South Wales and held meetings for days on end in tents, halls, and in the pits during the dinner hours. Hers seemed to the poor miners as the form and voice of an angel (King, *Woman,* p. 425).

Isabel became president of the British Woman's Temperance Association in 1890, and many attributed her sympathy with the outcasts of society due to her ostracism from society after her marriage failed. By 1891 Lady Somerset had found acceptance in British reform circles.

Isabel visited America to attend a convention of the World's Woman's Christian Temperance Union (WWCTU). At that time she met Frances Willard, with whom she became fast friends and associates in the temperance movement. Lady Somerset took Frances Willard back with her to England for a much needed rest.

Lady Henry Somerset gave her life in service for her fellow man. Hers might have been a life of ease and selfish idleness, yet she chose to give herself untiringly to the betterment of her fellow human beings.

Anna Jarvis
Founder of Mother's Day

"A printed card means nothing except that you are too lazy to write to the woman who has done more for you than anyone in the world. And candy! You take a box to Mother - and then eat most of it yourself. A pretty sentiment." These words came from the Mouth of Anna Jarvis, Founder of Mother's Day (*Women's Voices, Anna Jarvis*).

Anna Marie Jarvis was born in Webster, West Virginia on May 1, 1864. According to historical records, at an early age, Anna heard her mother express hope that a memorial would be established for all mothers, living and dead. Anna's mother, Mrs. Anna M. Jarvis, had been instrumental in developing "Mothers Friendship Day" which was part of the healing process of the Civil War. Mrs. Jarvis had established a group of Mother's Day Work Clubs in Webster, Grafton, Fetterman, Pruntytown, and Philippi, (West Virginia) to improve health and hygiene practices and conditions before the beginning of the Civil War. During the Civil War, Mrs. Anna Jarvis urged the Mother's Day Work Clubs to declare their neutrality and to help both Union and Confederate soldiers. The clubs treated the wounded and fed and clothed soldiers that were stationed in the area.

Near the end of the war, the Jarvis family moved to the larger town of Grafton, West Virginia. Naturally, as West Virginians fought on both sides during the war (the state, incorporated into the Union in 1864, was part of Virginia before the war), there was great tension when the soldiers returned home. In the summer of 1865, Anna Jarvis organized a Mother's Friendship Day at the courthouse in Pruntytown to bring together soldiers and neighbors of all political beliefs. The event was a complete success promoting friendship and peace. Mother's Friendship Day became an annual event for several years.

After the death of her father in 1902, Anna --along with her mother and sister, Lillie -- moved to Philadelphia to reside with her brother, Claude. It wasn't long after that her mother died. When Mrs. Jarvis died on May 9, 1905, her daughter Anna was resolved to honor her. She also felt that even though the U.S. was a hard working, industrialized nation, the adult children of her generation had become negligent in the treatment of their parents. In 1907, Miss Anna began a campaign to establish a national Mother's Day. Anna led a small tribute to her mother at Andrews Methodist Church on May 12 of that year, the 2nd anniversary of her mother's death. It was from that moment on that she dedicated her life to establishing a nationally recognized Mother's Day. By the next year, Mother's Day was also celebrated in her own city of Philadelphia.

Miss Jarvis and her supporters began to write to godly ministers, evangelists, businessmen, and politicians in their crusade to establish a national Mother's Day. This campaign was a success. By 1911, Mother's Day was celebrated in almost every state in the Union. In 1914, President Woodrow Wilson made the official announcement proclaiming Mother's Day as a national holiday that was to be held each year on the second Sunday of May.

The one-woman crusade of Anna Jarvis is often overlooked in history books. Women during the early 1900s were engaged in so many other reform efforts that the history behind Mother's Day is often neglected. It is likely, however, that it was these other reforms and the avenues they opened for women that paved the way for Anna Jarvis to succeed in her campaign for Mother's Day.

It must be noted that, while Miss Jarvis spent most of her adult life striving to create a special day to honor mothers, in the end, she was disappointed with the way Mother's Day turned out. As the popularity of the holiday grew, so did its commercialization. What she had intended as a day of sentiment quickly turned into a day of profit. In the end, shortly before her death, Anna Jarvis told a reporter that she was sorry she ever started Mother's Day.

Patricia R. Chadwick

Clara Barton
Angel of the Battlefield

When we think of the many and diverse benevolent undertakings and achievements of Clara Barton, one marvels at her seemingly iron and will and devotion to human welfare. In her long career she held a variety of positions. She began as a teacher in New Jersey and went on to become a battlefield nurse, lecturer and, perhaps her greatest work, organizer and president of the American Red Cross.

Despite life-threatening conditions, Clara provided supplies and care to troops in the American Civil War. She also served in the hospitals during the Franco-German War, was superintendent of the reformatory prison for women at Sherborn, Massachusetts, and was president of the American Red Cross Society. Clara ministered to those who suffered from the effects of a variety of disasters. In all her work, Clara Barton gave of herself, unceasingly, without reservation, until relief had been given.

Clara was born on Christmas day in 1821 in North Oxford, Massachusetts into a family of five children to the Captain Stephen Barton and his wife Sarah. While her father was a farmer, he had also been a soldier. His stories of his army experiences instilled in Clara a lifelong interest in the military.

Early in her life, her gift of mercy was revealed. She would often play nurse, taking care of pets that were sick or injured. When she was eleven, her brother, David, was badly injured in an accident and Clara attended him night and day for nearly two (King, *Woman,* p. 437). The lessons she learned in this experience were useful to her later work.

A shy girl, Clara sought to overcome her shyness by entering the field of teaching. She taught school until her health failed. For rest and restoration she went to Washington, DC, and after a time was appointed to a position in the Patent Office. Clara found this job unfulfilling and left that position to go to the front to minister, without pay, to the sick and wounded soldiers of the Civil War, earning her the well deserved title of "Angel of the Battlefield".

Another invaluable service initiated by Clara was the establishing of a Bureau of Records of missing men of the Union Army, compiled from prison and hospital rolls and burial lists. To this work she gave four years of her time and expended more than $10,000 of her own money. Congress voted to reimburse her, but she declined remuneration for her services.

She was in Europe when the Franco-German war broke out and was immediately asked to go to the front lines to assist in caring for the wounded. In recognition of her services, she received numerous badges of honor from nobility and royalty. Though broken in health from all her work on behalf of others, Clara returned to America and became the first president of

Patricia R. Chadwick

the American Association of the Red Cross in 1881. She
served in this capacity until 1904 when she retired to her home
at Glen Echo, Maryland. She died on April 12, 1912 at the
age of 91.

Helen Miller Gould
Philanthropist

Helen Miller Gould was an American philanthropist that gave not only of her money, but also of herself, to the work of relieving distress and making the world a better place. She achieved extended fame through her benefactions for charitable and educational uses. Helen earned the friendship of those she helped by giving her personal compassion and intelligent interest with her gifts of money.

Helen Miller Gould was born in New York City, the eldest daughter of the famous financier, Jay Gould. She was educated by private instructors under the careful eye of her father. So that she might have a knowledge of business for the management of her own affairs, her father enrolled her in the New York Law University. In 1913, Helen married Finley J. Shepard.

As previously mentioned, Helen was very generous with her money. At one time she gave $250,000 for the Library of the University of the City of New York, and followed that with another $60,000 at a later time. For the St. Louis cyclone sufferers in 1896, she donated $100,000. Rutgers, Vassar, and Mount Holyoke Colleges all received generous gifts as well as the Engineering School of the University of the City of New

York. The Naval Branch of the Young Men's Christian Association near Brooklyn Navy Yard received $50,000 and Miss Gould gave "Woody Crest", a home for crippled children $150,000 (Adleman, *Famous Women,* p. 309).

When the Windsor Hotel, opposite her home in New York, was burned, she, herself, ministered to the firemen and others in the rescue work. The firemen showed their deep gratitude by preparing an address and sending it by the hands of a committee of ten, representing a constituency of more than eighteen hundred.

One project of Helen's that was interesting, if not really charitable, was the Hall of Fame for Great Americans, which is still found on the campus of Bronx Community College, which is part of the City University of New York. Located in University Heights, the campus was originally part of the uptown campus of New York University. Helen provided the original funding for this memorial and set some conditions regarding who might be admitted. Helen's condition was that only people that had been dead ten years or more were to be eligible. The time period was extended to 25 years in 1922. Even though 50 names were to be inscribed in 1900, only 29 were elected from more than 1,000 nominations. Being in this Hall of Fame was a great honor.

Perhaps Helen's greatest work was her patriotic efforts during the Spanish-American War. At the outbreak of the war with Spain she gave $100,000 to the United States Government for relief of the soldiers at Camp Wycoff, Long

Island.   On December 5, 1898, General Joseph Wheeler, through Congressman Stallings, introduced in the House a bill providing that, in recognition of the patriotic devotion and bounteous benevolence of Miss Gould to the soldiers of the Unites States during the Spanish-American War, the thanks of Congress be offered and an appropriate medal be prepared, the same to be presented to Helen by the President.

Patricia R. Chadwick

Francis Powers Cobb
Founder of Ragged Schools

Frances Power Cobbe was a nineteenth century feminist, philanthropist, theological and social writer, and strong supporter of women's rights, particularly the woman's suffrage movement. She was associated with Mary Carpenter in the founding of "Ragged Schools", taking an active part in the movement for the restoration of neglected children. She was also well known as an anti-vivisectionist, condemning animal experimentation.

Francis was born in Newbridge, near Dublin, Ireland and was a descendant of Charles Cobbe, Archbishop of Dublin. When she was quite young, her mother died. This led Francis in search of the meaning of life and whether or not there was an after-life. This search led her to inquire of Theodore Parker, the brilliant rationalist, social reformer, and Unitarian clergyman, concerning the future life. Parker's thinking influenced her own beliefs from that time on and under his tutelage she became a strong Theist and a Unitarian. In fact, she was so intimate with his work that she edited 14 volumes published between 1863 and 1871.

Frances was a student of history, philosophy, and astronomy. Her feminist tendencies led her to become a champion of higher education for women.   She was also an author of several books, including *Studies New and Old of Ethical and Social Subjects*, *Broken Lights,* which was a statement of the doctrines of different divisions of the English Church, *Essay on Intuitive Morals*, probably her most well written work, *The Duties of Woman*, and *Darwinism in Morals*. Her first published work; *The Intuitive Theory of Morals* was published anonymously in 1855.

Frances traveled in Italy and the East and upon returning wrote *Cities of the Past* and *Italics*. Later Miss Cobbe became interested in social questions and philanthropic work and she wrote many books on similar subjects, including *Criminals, Idiots, Women and Minors* in 1869 and *Scientific Spirit of the Age* in 1888. Early in her career she assisted at the Redhouse Reformatory, London. She also was a strong supporter and campaigner for the Matrimonial Causes Act, 1878. Along with her rationalistic writings on religious themes, she contributed to the press and personally worked in the behalf of the poor and friendless.

4

Suffragists

Lucy Stone

Anna Shaw

Lucretia Mott

Elizabeth Cady Stanton

Carrie Chapman Catt

Susan B. Anthony

Mary Livermore

Lucy Stone

Lucy Stone was a women's right advocate that worked unceasingly to improve the condition of women in the 1800's. While she is noted for many things, Lucy is probably best known for being the first woman to retain her own name after marriage.

Lucy Stone was born near West Brookfield, Massachusetts on August 13, 1818, the eighth of nine children. Her childhood was spent watching her father rule the household with an "iron hand". Her lot in life was one of toil from childhood. Although she had to perform the usual duties of a farmer's daughter, all the time she was thinking and questioning. Her soul rebelled at the unequal lot of woman especially concerning education and wages (Bolton, *Famous Leaders*, p. 212)

Lucy was a bright girl, but received little formal education during her childhood. While her two brothers received financial help from her father to go to college, when Lucy desired to do the same her father told her she was crazy. Few women of her day went to college or were educated above simple reading, writing, and counting. He refused to help her.

Though she had no support from her family, Lucy was determined that SHE WOULD go to college. She picked berries and saved the money earned. She gathered chestnuts and with the money bought books. When she was sixteen, she was offered a job teaching school at the wage of one dollar a week. With time, her wages increased and when she was earning sixteen dollars per month, it was thought remarkable for a woman. When her brother was sick, she took over teaching in his school while he recovered. His wages were thirty dollars per month, but the committee gave her only sixteen because they felt it "was enough for a woman". While these things brought bitterness to her heart, she used them to spur her on to fight for the rights of women.

When she was twenty-five years old she had earned money enough to enter Oberlin College. Oberlin, which was in Ohio, was the only college at the time that would admit women. She earned her way in part by tutoring and doing housework. Lucy had to live very frugally to afford her education. In fact, in four years time, she only had one new dress.

After graduating from Oberlin, Lucy became involved in several reform movements of the day. She was a prominent abolitionist and her life work became seeking reform for both the slave and the woman. Lucy received much opposition and insults, but she persevered. She worked for woman suffrage in Colorado and in 1893 was able to see her work bear fruit in the state's constitutional amendment giving woman the same rights as men in exercising the election franchise.

Many sought her hand in marriage, but she refused them all. Finally, Henry Blackwell, a fellow abolitionist, won her friendship and trust, and finally her hand in marriage. They were married in 1855 when Lucy was thirty-seven years old. They agreed before the marriage that Lucy would retain her maiden name and be known simply as Lucy Stone.

Patricia R. Chadwick

Anna Howard Shaw

Anna Howard Shaw was one of the first women given a license to preach in the Methodist Episcopal church. Her lifetime accomplishments include not only her work in religion, but in the fields of women's rights, medicine, and public speaking, which resulted in her fame worldwide.

Anna Howard Shaw was born in England on February 14, 1847. When she was four years old the Shaw family moved from England to America, where they lived in Massachusetts. In 1859 they settled in the wilderness of Green Township, Mecosta County, near Big Rapids, Michigan. They lived on an isolated, rundown farm that required much work before it would become productive. After living there only a short time, her father left her mother and the children alone on the farm and returned to Massachusetts to work. He left them in a really sorry state. The farmhouse was a cabin with only holes for doors and windows and the fields were full of tree stumps. Her father's absence caused the mother to have a nervous breakdown and her oldest brother was in poor health, forcing 12-year-old Anna to care for the farm by clearing the land, planting crops, and finishing off the cabin along with caring for the family.

Anna only received two years of formal schooling as a youth, which she supplemented with her own reading. When she was fourteen years old she felt the call to preach and at the age of fifteen she began to teach school in a frontier schoolhouse. Eventually she went on to attend high school in Big Rapids, Michigan and then on to study at Albion College. Having an adventurous spirit and thirst for knowledge, Anna later studied at Boston University where she earned a theology degree in 1878. She has the distinction of being the second woman to graduate from Boston University School of Theology, but the New England Conference of the Methodist Episcopal Church refused her ordination. She did, however, receive ordination by the New York Conference of the Methodist Protestant Church in 1880, becoming the first woman to be ordained in any branch of Methodism (Adelman, *Famous Women,* p.258).

While serving in East Dennis, Massachusetts in the Wesleyan Methodist Church, Anna continued her education and earned a medical degree from Boston University. When she was thirty-nine years old she branched out from the field of pastoral and healing ministries to speak out for social justice concerns, organizing and lecturing throughout the world for the causes such as temperance, peace, and women's rights. During her lifetime she gave more than 10,000 lectures worldwide.

In 1892, when Susan B. Anthony became president of the newly formed National American Woman Suffrage Association (NAWSA), Anna became vice president. In 1904, Anna became the president of the NAWSA. Throughout this time frame she was a well-known figure in demonstrations, conferences, congressional hearings, and lecture circuits. She spoke in every state of the United States and she also performed home-front war work during World War I, receiving a Distinguished Service Medal by the U.S. Congress.

In the midst of a successful speaking career, Anna Howard Shaw fell ill and died in her home in Moylan, Pennsylvania on July 2, 1919. She will forever be remembered for her enduring legacy resulting from her leadership in the women's suffrage movement.

Lucretia Mott

Lucretia Coffin Mott was a nineteenth century Quaker minister and reformer. She is well known for her work in moral reform including temperance and abolition. She is best known, however, for her work in the Women's Rights Movement of her day and especially for her work in organizing the first Women's Rights Convention in New York State in 1848.

Lucretia Coffin was born in 1793 on the island of Nantucket, Massachusetts. Early on she was impressed by her mother's active role in the community and church congregation, or Society as Quakers called it, to which they belonged. As a rule, Quakers believed in the equality of all people, no matter what the race or the sex, which made them very active in moral reform, including abolition and women's rights. The Mott family moved to Boston in 1804 and Lucretia was sent to a Quaker boarding school in Poughkeepsie, New York. Lucretia was well educated and went on to teach in that same school at the age of fifteen.

In 1809 she moved to Philadelphia with her family where she married James Mott, a fellow teacher at the Poughkeepsie school who had recently joined her father's hardware company. They were a fine match and their marriage has been spoken of as one of the most perfect the world has ever seen.

In 1821, Lucretia became a Quaker minister, noted for her intellectual ability, sweetness of disposition, and speaking ability. In 1827 she and James changed their religious affiliation to that of the Hicksite Quakers, a more liberal branch of the Society of Friends and became deeply involved in the abolitionist movement. She soon became known for her persuasive speeches against slavery. Like many Hicksites, she refused to use cotton cloth, cane sugar, and other products produced by slaves. In 1833, Lucretia helped form the American Anti-Slavery Society and the Philadelphia Female Anti-Slavery Society. In 1937 she helped organize the Anti-Slavery Convention of American Women. With the support of her husband, the Mott's frequently sheltered runaway slaves. While she was active in her role as a minister and in the cause of abolition, she was always first a wife, mother, and homemaker.

In 1840, Lucretia was sent with other women as delegates to the World's Anti-Slavery Convention in London. The men in charge of the meeting, however, were opposed to public speaking and action by women and refused to seat the women delegates. This was an outrage to Lucretia and other women. It was here, while seated in the segregated women's section at these meetings, that she met Elizabeth Cady Stanton and their conversations at this meeting are often credited as being the stimuli for the first Women's Rights Convention to be held eight years later (Adelman, *Famous Women*, p. 167).

In 1848, Mott and Stanton called the first Women's Rights

Convention in Seneca Falls, N.Y., where Elizabeth lived. It was here that the Women's Rights Movement was born. After this first convention, Lucretia became increasingly dedicated to women's rights and began to speak widely for it.

Lucretia Mott was a social reformer and a philanthropist. She was a woman of modesty and courage, gentleness and force, with a sharp intellect and a great heart. She worked quietly but mightily for God and humanity.

Elizabeth Cady Stanton

Elizabeth Cady Stanton was born in 1815, the daughter of Judge Cady, of Johnstown, New York. She was raised in a community where most of the people were Scotch and where the idea of a woman's place and ability was very limited in scope. Elizabeth had an older brother, upon whom her father had set his hopes and gave an excellent education. This brother, however, died just after he graduated from Union College, when Elizabeth was only ten years old.

Elizabeth saw her father's grief and disappointment and was determined to fill her brother's place. By his own words, he had made it clear to her that a girl was not as worthwhile to him as a boy. She applied herself to her studies and excelled in Greek, Latin, and mathematics, hoping to please her father and proving to him that a girl could be as good a student as a boy. But the expected commendation did not come. She then took up additional studies and prepared herself to enter Union College, but she was refused because of her sex.

Upon this denial, Elizabeth entered the Troy Female Seminary and received and excellent education, the finest available to women at that time. After a few years at Troy Female Seminary, Elizabeth returned home and spent seven years studying law in her father's office.

In time, Elizabeth met and married Henry Stanton, an activist in the anti-slavery cause. The word "obey" was omitted from the wedding ceremony at her insistence. The couple attended the World's Anti-Slavery Convention in London on their wedding tour. Here Mrs. Stanton met Lucretia Mott, who, with others, had been sent as delegates from the United States. During the convention, the women delegates were not seated or allowed to vote. This convinced Elizabeth that women should hold a convention for their own rights (Adelman, *Famous Women*, p. 172).

Upon her return to America, Mrs. Stanton was instrumental in calling the first Women's Rights Convention. The idea first came about in 1847 after her move to Seneca Falls, where she was isolated and increasingly exhausted by a growing family. Her father, hearing of this, feared she had become insane and visited her to discourage her from undertaking such a project.

Finally, in 1848, she met with Lucretia Mott and three other Quaker women in nearby Waterloo, NY. Together they issued the call for the first Women's Rights Convention. At the convention, Stanton introduced the resolution, "That it is the duty of the women of this country to secure to themselves the sacred right of the elective franchise." (James, *Notable Women*, p. 343).

Mrs. Stanton was far in advance of her age and was subjected to both opposition and ridicule, but she continued to be an educator of public opinion and a champion of women's rights. Though she died before seeing her dream come to fruition, her work was instrumental in bringing about the Nineteenth Amendment in 1920, which gave women the vote.

Patricia R. Chadwick

Carrie Chapman Catt

Carrie Chapman Catt was a key coordinator of the suffrage movement and skillful political strategist that played a leading role in gaining the vote for women in 1920. Her talent for public speaking and her organizational skills put her at the top of the National American Woman Suffrage Association (NAWSA), enabling her to put her secret "winning plan" into affect, securing voting rights for women by the passage of the nineteenth amendment. More than any other woman, except for Susan B. Anthony, Carrie Chapman Catt was responsible for the amendment's passage in 1920.

Carrie Chapman Catt was born as Carrie Lane on January 9, 1859 in Ripon, Wisconsin. She was the daughter of Lucius and Maria Clinton Lane. Her parents both graduated from Potsdam Academy, Potsdam, New York. Her parents moved west in 1855 and started their family after settling in Wisconsin. When Carrie was seven years old, her family moved to Iowa where she spent the rest of her childhood. While in Iowa, Carrie began preparatory school where she trained as a teacher. She also studied law briefly and was appointed a high school principal a year after she graduated from Iowa State College.

In February of 1885, Carrie married Leo Chapman, editor

and publisher of the *Mason City Republican*. The couple moved to California, but Leo died shortly thereafter of typhoid fever, leaving Carrie to make her own living. She found work as a newspaper reporter, becoming the San Francisco's first female news reporter.

Carrie soon joined the suffrage movement as a lecturer, moving back to Iowa where she joined the Iowa Woman Suffrage Association. In 1890 she was elected delegate at the newly formed National American Woman Suffrage Association and that same year she married wealthy engineer George W. Catt. Carrie had originally met Catt in college and then met him again while she was in San Francisco. Before the marriage they signed a prenuptial agreement, which guaranteed her time for her suffrage work. They agreed to two months in the spring and two in the fall for her suffrage work. George was very supportive in her efforts towards woman suffrage. They had no children.

Carrie became an excellent public speaker and organizer. Her hard work, writing and speaking engagements established Carrie's reputation as a leading suffragist. Carrie worked with the NAWSA from 1890 to 1900 when she succeeded Susan B. Anthony as president of the group. From that time on she primarily focused on lecturing, planning campaigns, organizing women, and gaining political knowledge and experience. She led the campaign to win women's suffrage with a federal amendment to the constitution in 1920.

In 1902 Catt helped organize the IWSA (International Woman Suffrage Alliance), but in 1904 she resigned the presidency from NAWSA to tend to her sick husband. Her husband died in October 1905 and she received another blow at the death of her friend and fellow worker Susan B. Anthony in 1906. After the death of Anthony, Carrie was encouraged by her doctors and friends to travel abroad. She spent the next nine years abroad as president of IWSA promoting equal-suffrage rights worldwide.

Upon returning to the United States in 1915, Catt resumed leadership of the NAWSA, which had become badly divided under the leadership of Anna Howard Shaw. Under the dynamic leadership of Carrie Chapman Catt, the NAWSA won the backing of the House of Representatives and the Senate as well as state support for the ratification of the amendment. On August 26, 1920 the Nineteenth Amendment officially became part of the U.S. Constitution, due to the tireless work of this great woman. Carrie Chapman Catt died of heart failure in New Rochelle, New York on March 9, 1946 at the age of eighty-six.

Susan B. Anthony

Susan B. Anthony is best known for her work in the Woman Suffrage Movement that began in the mid 1800's. Along with Elizabeth Cady Stanton, her name is almost synonymous with "Women's Rights". For most of her adult life Susan gave herself unceasingly to the work of improving the circumstances of women in this nation. While, in Christian circles, there seems to be a stigma attached to those who have supported the Woman's Rights Movement, it is a little known fact that it was her religious heritage that led Susan to champion the cause for women's rights in 19th century America.

Susan Brownell Anthony was born on February 15, 1820 to Daniel and Lucy Read Anthony in Adams, Massachusetts. Daniel Anthony came from a long line of Quakers, or Society of Friends, which was their preferred name, dating back to the time the sect was introduced in America during the mid-seventeenth century. Though she was a Christian woman, her mother was not a Quaker, fearing she could not measure up to the strictness of the sect, yet she regularly attended services with her family and held many of the same beliefs. The Anthony children were all were all members of the Society of Friends and participated fully in their meetings.

Being raised as a Quaker was very significant in shaping

Susan's attitudes and outlook on life. While growing up in the Society of Friends, she was taught that each person had an "inner light", a kind of spiritual nerve center, through which God revealed Himself. To the Quakers, God was no respecter of persons. They believed that God created all people as equal and that there was no distinction between male, female or between races. Their belief that all people were created equal led the many Quakers to take a stand for the equality of all people.

Susan was raised with the ideal that women were equal with men and should have the same rights and opportunities. She was given a good education because of her parents' religious conviction that young women, as well as young men, should be properly educated. The idea of giving a young lady any education beyond the bare essentials was not looked upon favorably by most people of that era. But the Quakers insisted on equal opportunities for all people, including women. In fact, her paternal grandmother and aunts all held high positions in the Society to which her family belonged. With this appraisal of women accepted as a matter of fact in her church and family circle, Susan took it for granted that it existed everywhere.

Her religious upbringing not only had an influence on Susan's ideals, but it also affected her actions. Quakers were very service- minded and believed in helping their fellowman and woman by providing for their human physical, social, and spiritual needs. It was her religious heritage that led Susan to be involved in a variety of social concerns.

As a young woman, Susan took up the causes of abolition, temperance, and the furtherance of women's rights with equal fervor. As she worked in these areas she regretfully realized that the majority of people in our nation did not hold her ideals of equality among all people that were taught to her as a child. She came up against such prejudice against women that she came to realize the only way that the plight of women would change was if women had the Vote. It was this realization that caused her to focus her energy on the Woman Suffrage Movement.

Susan B. Anthony had high ideals and a great vision. Many things shaped her into the great woman that she was, but nothing influenced her more than the religious principles taught to her as a child. It was her belief that all people were created equal before God that empowered her to become the defender of equal rights and a principal leader in the Woman Suffrage movement.

Mary Livermore

Mary Livermore was an American journalist, philanthropist, and lecturer during the nineteenth century. During the Civil War, she worked in hospitals, was a correspondent for numerous journals, an author, and edited her husband's newspaper. She was the only woman reporter at Lincoln's nomination. After the Civil War she was active in temperance, suffrage, and abolitionist movements.

Born Mary Ashton Rice in Boston on December 19, 1820, Mary was of Welsh descent. She graduated from the Boston public schools at fourteen and then attended the Female Seminary in Charlestown, Massachusetts. She graduated from there in two years instead of the allotted four, and upon graduation became a member of the faculty, teaching Latin and French.

In 1845 Mary married Rev. Daniel P. Livermore. Her husband was called to Chicago to become manager and editor of the publication, *The New Covenant* and Mary became his associate on the paper and was an invaluable asset to him in this work.

When the Civil War broke out, Mary went to the front lines as a nurse and was often under enemy fire. There was strong prejudice against women as army nurses, and she experienced much opposition in her work. Mrs. Livermore also founded The Sanitary Commission and the association was largely indebted to her for its organized efforts. When money came in slowly, she instituted the great Chicago Soldiers' Fair, which raised $100,000. As an author she wrote *My Story of the War* that reached a sale of more than fifty thousand copies.

At the close of the war she turned her energies in the direction of women's rights. In 1868 she organized the Chicago Woman Suffrage Convention and established "The Agitator", a feminist journal, for the advocacy of temperance reform and woman suffrage. In 1870 *The Woman's Journal* was started and she became the editor, her own paper becoming absorbed in the new journal. She also was one of the leaders in the Women's Christian Temperance Union.

For thirteen years Mary Livermore delivered on an average of one hundred and fifty lectures per year. She spoke on a variety of topics including biography, history, politics, religion, temperance, and other reforms. She died on May 23, 1905.

5

Queen of Sheba
The Queen Who Sought Wisdom

Eleanor of Aquitaine
Wife of Louis VII of France

Elizabeth of Hungary
Saintly Princess

Catherine of Valois
Queen of Henry V of England

Lady Jane Grey
Nine Days Queen of England

Mary I
Bloody Mary

Catherine de'Medici
Famous Mother of Kings

Elizabeth I
Last of the Tudor Line

Mary Queen of Scots
Queen of Scotland

Mary II
Co-Regent of England with William III

Queen Anne
Queen of England

Catherine I
Empress of Russia

Patricia R. Chadwick

Queen Victoria
Beloved Queen

Empress Eugenie
Empress of France

Tsz Hsi An
Empress Dowager of China

Queen of Sheba
The Queen Who Sought Wisdom

Sheba was the name of a great South Arabian kingdom whose name meant "Host of Heaven and peace". Located in southwest Arabia on the eastern tip of the Red Sea, Sheba occupied 483,000 square miles and many historians believe that it included the land of Ethiopia, on the western end of the Red Sea. Sheba was a wealthy country rich in gold and other precious stones as well as incense and spices that were much sought after by neighboring countries. She also had an advanced irrigation procedures and hydraulic power. It's peoples built dams and large earthen wells that also contributed to their thriving agriculture and exotic gardens. Trade caravans frequently traveled to Sheba to trade for her goods.

The Sabaean people were Semitic in origin and believed to have been the descendents of Cush in the Bible. They have been described as a tall and impressive people. Because of isolation, Sheba was unable to be invaded and was independent and at peace with neighboring kingdoms for nearly 500 years during the 11th and 10th centuries B.C.

The Queen of Sheba no doubt thought it wise to keep on good terms with Israel, which was rapidly rising in power. She was also undoubtedly curious regarding the stories told of the wisdom and regal splendor of Israel's king, Solomon. She prepared her royal caravan and started on her thousand-mile journey. Solomon was accustomed to royal gifts from surrounding nations but the camels laden with the choicest of spices from the land of spices surprised even the king. The Bible states that "There came no more such abundance of spices as these which the queen of Sheba gave to King Solomon" (1 Kings 10:10), and the hundred and twenty talents of gold, over fifteen million dollars, was a gift that even the wealthiest of kings could not ignore.

We may presume that Solomon and his people had not held the people of Arabia in high esteem. They had neither the history nor the deeds of Egypt and the Far East to boast of, but they had gold mines, which made that metal an abundant commodity. The coming of that caravan to Jerusalem changed the opinion of the Israelites regarding that great south land.

The Queen of Sheba, who brought surprises, found more surprises herself. Day after day she listened to Solomon's words, putting to him hard questions in philosophy and religion, especially seeking information concerning his God. She gazed on the splendid architecture of palace and temple, and at last was led to exclaim, "It was a true report that I heard in mine own land of thy acts and of thy wisdom. Howbeit, I believed not the words until I came and mine eyes had seen it; and behold the half was not told me!" (King, *Woman,* p. 60).

Legend has it that King Solomon and the Queen of Sheba fell in love and were married. Supposedly together they had one son who became emperor of Ethiopia and started the Solomonic Jewish dynasty in that country.

Eleanor of Aquitaine
Wife of Louis VII of France

Eleanor of Aquitaine was one of the most fascinating personalities of Medieval Europe. In her youth she was remarkably beautiful, and in her later years her showed evidences of a noble disposition. She is one of the few women of ancient times who have atoned for an ill-spent youth by a wise and benevolent old age. Eleanor of Aquitaine ranks among the greatest of female rulers.

Born around 1122, Eleanor was the daughter of William X, duke of Aquitaine and Count of Poitiers. Upon her father's death in 1137, Eleanor inherited Aquitaine and Poitiers. That same year, at the age of 15, she also married Louis VII, King of France, bringing to the union her vast possessions from the River Loire to the Pyrenees.

Eleanor was a very intelligent woman; many considered her superior in intellect than her husband. She was also very courageous and passionate. In fact, Eleanor and her retinue, dressed in battle attire, joined Louis VII on the Second Crusade. While the church may have been glad to receive her fighting vassals, they were less than pleased when they learned that Eleanor and 300 of her ladies planned to go along (King, *Woman,* p. 197).

On their journey to the Holy Land, they first stopped at Antioch, where Eleanor's uncle, Raymond of Tripoli, had been appointed prince of the city. She renewed her friendship with her kin, spending so much time with him that Louis grew jealous. When Louis prepared to leave for Jerusalem, Eleanor refused to go with him, threatening a divorce. Louis, however, took her by force. The expedition failed and both returned to France in separate ships. While the marriage continued for a time, the couple finally separated after the birth of their second daughter. The marriage was annulled in 1152 and Eleanor's vast estates reverted to her control.

Six weeks after her divorce, Eleanor married Henry, duke of Normandy, who soon afterwards became Henry II of England. During her marriage to Henry, Eleanor continued to rule Aquitaine, which consisted of Guienne and Gascony. The couple had eight children including Richard Coeur de Lion (Richard the Lionhearted), who ruled England from 1189 - 1199 and John Lackland who ruled from 1199 - 1216.

Eleanor was very jealous of her second husband, Henry II. In 1173, she incited her sons to rebel against their father, giving them military support. The revolt failed and Eleanor was thrown into prison, where she remained for sixteen years, until her husband's death. In 1189 she was released from prison by order of her son, Richard, when he took the throne. Richard then proceeded to place her at the head of the government.

While she undoubtedly underwent much deprivation during her imprisonment, she did not, when she obtained power, use it to punish her enemies, but rather devoted herself to deeds of mercy and piety, going from city to city, setting free all persons confined for violating the game laws, which in the latter part of Henry's life, were cruelly enforced. In 1202, Eleanor retired to the monastery at Fontevrault, Anjou, where she died in 1204. She goes down in history as one of the greatest female sovereigns of all time

Patricia R. Chadwick

Elizabeth of Hungary
Saintly Princess

Elizabeth of Hungary was a Hungarian princess and philanthropist of the thirteenth century who was concerned for the relief of the poor and sick. With consent of her husband she used her dowry money to aid the needy in her land.

Elizabeth was born at Presburg in 1207 the daughter of Andreas II, king of Hungary. At the age of four she was affianced to the Landgraf of Thuringia, Louis IV, who was himself an infant. She was then brought to his court in the Wartburg, near Eisenach, to be educated under the watchful eyes of her future parents-in-law. She early displayed a passion for the severities of the Christian life and as she grew in age, she also grew in piety. She hated pomp and ambition, cultivated humility, and exhibited much self-denying benevolence. Her conduct, even as a girl, amazed the Thuringian court.

When she was but fourteen years old, her marriage to Louis IV took place and together they had three children. In spite of her position at court, Elizabeth began to lead a simple life and devoted herself to works of charity. Louis admired Elizabeth for her long prayers and ceaseless almsgiving, for he himself was attracted to this mode of life. He was inclined to religion and encouraged her in her exemplary life. It was he who encouraged her to use her dowry money for the relief of the poor and the sick. In 1226, while Louis was away in Italy, Elizabeth sold her jewels and established a hospital at the foot of her castle where she nursed the sick herself and opened the royal granaries to feed the hungry, knowing she would have her husband's approval.

Great misfortunes soon befell the saintly Elizabeth. In 1227 tragedy first struck with the death of Louis while fighting with the Crusaders. After the death of her husband, Louis's brother deprived Elizabeth of her regency and she was expelled from her home at Wartburg on the grounds that she wasted the treasure of the state by her extravagant giving to charities. She at last found refuge in the church, where her first care was to thank God that he had judged her worthy to suffer.

When the warriors who attended her husband in the Crusade returned from the East, they found Elizabeth and listened to her recount all her sufferings at the hands of her in-laws. Steps were taken to restore the princess with her sovereign rights. She declined the throne, however, but did accept a stipend of 500 marks a year.

She became a Franciscan tertiary and devoted the remainder of her life to nursing and charity and ascetic living. She put on a nun's raiment and took up her residence in a cottage at the foot of the hill on which stood her castle of Marburg, giving her life to ceaseless devotions, almsgiving, and mortifications. All her revenues were given to the poor and what she required for personal expenditures for herself

and her three children she earned with her own hands.
She died November 19, 1231 (King, *Woman,* p. 204).

Catherine of Valois
Queen of Henry V of England

Catherine of Valois, was the youngest child of Charles VI of France and Isabelle of Bavaria. She was born on October 27, 1401, at the Hotel de St. Paul in Paris during her father's period of insanity. Catherine was almost entirely neglected during her childhood due to her father's frequent bouts of insanity and her mother's selfish indifference. While the king was ill, her mother joined the king's brother, the Duke of Orleans, in pilfering the revenues of the household. When Charles recovered, Isabelle fled with he Duke of Orleans to Milan, followed by her children, who were pursued and brought back by the Duke of Burgundy.

Catherine was educated in the convent at Poissy, where her sister Marie was consecrated. When she was twelve years old, King Henry V of England renewed negotiations begun by his father, Henry IV for the hand of Catherine. Henry demanded a large dowry and restoration of former English lands and when they were rejected it led to war. Henry invaded France and forced compliance with his terms. After signing the Treaty of Troyes, Henry V married Catherine in Troyes, France in June of 1420. The Treaty not only restored to England the land of Normandy and Aquitaine, but also gave Henry the regency of France during the reign of Charles VII, because he was again insane, and the right to succeed to the

French throne after Charles's death, to the exclusion of Catherine's brother and three older sisters. Catherine was crowned in Westminster Abbey in February 1421 and gave birth to a son, Henry VI at Windsor in December of that year, while Henry was in France. The queen joined her husband in Paris in 1422, leaving her infant son in England, and was with him when he died at the castle of Vincennes, in August 1422. She returned to London and resided first at Windsor Castle then at Baynard's Castle, London.

Some years later Catherine married Owen Tudor, an officer of Welsh descent, who was clerk of the queen's wardrobe. This marriage was kept secret for several years because English Parliament forbade her marriage without consent of king and council. They had three sons and two daughters, one of which died in infancy. While they lived together, Catherine was a devoted mother and wife and lived very happily. In 1436, when the marriage was found out, Owen Tudor was imprisoned and Catherine was removed to Bermondsey Abbey, London. Being torn from her children was an act of cruelty that probably hastened her death. Catherine died in the care of pious nuns who did their best to comfort the Queen in her last days.

Lady Jane Grey
Nine-Day Queen of England

Lady Jane Grey was born at Brodgate, Leicestershire, England, in October 1537. She was the oldest daughter of Henry Grey, Marquis of Dorset, who became Duke of Suffolk in 1551 and of Lady Frances Brandon.

Lady Jane was brought up in an abusive household, with every petty fault punished with physical punishment. But her tutor, Aylmer, which afterwards became Bishop of London, was very fond of her and was gentle with her. Under his tutorship she made great progress, especially in the languages of Latin, Greek, French, Italian, and Hebrew.

Jane was an avid reader and given more to academics than recreation. Often, while the family was off hunting, she could be found reading classic literature in the original languages. She also sang and played musical instruments quite well and was accomplished in other feminine virtues.

In 1553, after the fall of the Duke of Somerset, the Duke of Northumberland, foreseeing the speedy death of the boy-king Edward VI, determined to change the succession and secure it to his own family. Lady Jane, not yet sixteen years old, was therefore married, strongly against her will, to Lord Dudley, Northumberland's fourth son, on May 21, 1553. On July 9, three days after Edward's death, the council informed her that she was named s his successor.

On the 19th of July, the brief usurpation over, she found herself a prisoner in the Tower and four months later, pleading guilty of high treason, she was sentenced to death. She spurned the idea of forsaking Protestantism to save her life, as was offered and bitterly condemned Northumberland's recantation. This, together with her father's participation in Wyatt's rebellion, sealed her doom and she was beheaded on Tower Hill, February 12, 1554.

From the scaffold she made a speech in which she said: "The fact indeed, against the queen's highness was unlawful, and the consenting to by me; but touching the procurement and desire thereof by me or on my behalf, I do wash my hands thereof in innocence.... I die a true Christian woman." (King, *Woman,* p. 251).

Elizabeth I
Last of the Tudor Line

Elizabeth, queen of England, and the last sovereign of the house of Tudor, was born at Greenwich, September 7, 1533. She was a daughter of Henry VIII and Anne Boleyn. Her childhood was passed in comparative quietness, and people who favored reformed religion educated her. She learned the Latin, Greek, French, and Italian languages with ease.

In 1554, Elizabeth was confined in the Tower by order of Queen Mary, who believed her to be implicated in Sir Thomas Wyatt's rebellion against the queen, and regarded her with jealousy because she was the favorite with the Protestant party. She narrowly escaped death, for some of the bishops and courtiers advised Mary to order her execution. After she had passed several months in the Tower, she was removed to Woodstock and appeased Mary by professing to be a Roman Catholic (Jackson, *Women Who Ruled,* p. 63).

On the death of Queen Mary, on November 17, 1558, Elizabeth ascended the throne, and the majority of the people rejoiced at her accession. She appointed William Cecil secretary of state, and Nicholas Bacon keeper of the great seal. She retained several Roman Catholics in her privy council, but she refused to hear mass in the royal chapel.

The Protestants were the majority in the Parliament, which met in 1559, and they abolished the mass, adopted the Thirty-Nine Articles as the religion of the State, and recognized the queen as the head of the Church. She declined an offer of marriage made to her by Philip of Spain. Her foreign policy was that of peace. She waged no war for conquest, but to promote the stability of her throne she aided the Protestant insurgents in Scotland, France, and the Netherlands, with money and troops.

In 1563, the Parliament, anxious that she should have an heir, entreated her to marry, but she returned an evasive answer, and would neither accept the hand of any of her suitors nor decide in favor of any claimant of the throne.

Mary, Queen of Scots, fleeing from her rebellious subjects, took refuge in England in 1568 and was detained as a prisoner by Elizabeth. Elizabeth regarded Mary as a dangerous rival, because the English Catholics wished to rais e her to the throne of England, and formed several plots and conspiracies to make that happen. Elizabeth had Mary beheaded on February 8, 1587. This was the darkest stain on the memory of Elizabeth.

Her reign was one of the most prosperous and glorious in English history. The Elizabethan age was almost unequaled in literature, and was illustrated by the genius of Shakespeare, Spenser, Bacon, Sidney, and Raleigh. Elizabeth died on March 24, 1603 and was succeeded by James VI of Scotland, who became James I of England.

Mary I
Bloody Mary

Mary I, Queen of England, which was given the nickname of "Bloody Mary", was born at Greenwich Palace, February 18, 1516. She was the daughter of Henry VIII and Catharine of Aragon. She was carefully educated in Spain, was an ardent Catholic, and became a proficient scholar in Latin, so that Erasmus commends her letters in that language.

Edward VI, her brother, died in 1553 and after disposing of Lady Jane Grey, her one threat to the throne, she became the first queen to rule of all of England in her own right (Jackson, *Women Who Ruled,* p.119). Upon her accession, she declared that she would not persecute her Protestant subjects, but in the following month, she restricted preaching, and in less than three months the Protestant bishops were excluded from the House of Lords and all the statutes of Edward VI regarding the Protestant religion were repealed.

Mary renewed the laws against heretics of the Catholic Church and began to enforce them. The shocking scenes, which followed, were horrifying. In three or four years, two hundred and seventy-seven people were burned at the stake (King, *Woman,* p. 250). The ruin of England seemed imminent, when in the summer of 1558, the queen became ill of a fever and she died at St. James Palace, on November 17.

To her, no doubt, the propagators of what she considered heresy were the enemies of mankind, and she had little cause to love them. Yet perhaps she hardly realized the full horror of what was done with her full approval.

Catherine de'Medici
Famous Mother of Kings

Catherine de'Medici, the wife of one king of France and the mother of three, was the daughter of Lorenzo de'Medici, Duke of Urbino, and was born at Florence in 1519. In her fourteenth year she was brought to France, and married to Henry, the second son of Francis I. The marriage was a part of the political schemes of her uncle, Pope Clement VII, but as he died soon after, she found herself friendless and neglected at the French court.

It wasn't until the accession of her eldest son, Francis II, in 1559, that she found some scope for her ambition. The Guises at this time were in power, and Catherine entered into a secret alliance with the Huguenots to oppose them. On the death of Francis II, in 1560, and accession of her second son, Charles IX, the government fell entirely into her hands.

She entered into a secret treaty with Spain for the annihilation of heretics and subsequently into a plot with the Guises, which resulted in the fearful massacre of St. Bartholomew's Day. This event brought the whole power of the state into the hands of the queen mother, who boasted of the deed to Roman Catholic governments, and excused it to Protestant ones Jackson, *Women Who Ruled, p.* 43).

Patricia R. Chadwick

About this time she succeeded, by money and intrigues, in getting her third son, afterwards Henry III elected to the Polish throne. But her arbitrary and tyrannical administration roused the opposition of a Roman Catholic party, at the head of which was her own fourth son, the Duke of Alencon. It is generally believed that she was privy to the plans that led to his death. Catherine was not well loved by her subjects and the queen mother died amidst strife and confusion of parties on January 5, 1589, unlamented.

Mary, Queen of Scots
Queen of Scotland

Mary Stuart, Queen of Scots, was born on December 8, 1542. She was well known for her beauty, her wit, and her learning, as well as her misfortunes. She was the daughter of James V of Scotland by Marie of Lorraine, a French princess of the family of Guise. Her father died a few days after her birth, and on September 9, 1543, she was crowned queen of Scotland.

In 1548 she was pledged in marriage to Francis, Dauphin of France, son of Henry II and Catharine de'Medic, and in the same year she was brought to France to be educated at the French court. When she grew up she added to a striking and fascinating personal beauty all the accomplishments and charms, which a perfect education can give.

Her marriage to Francis took place on April 24, 1558, in the Church of Notre Dame, and when Mary I of England died in the same year, she opposed the crowning of Elizabeth I.

On July 10, 1559, Henry II died and was succeeded by Francis II. Mary thus became Queen of France, but Francis died December 5, 1560. She was childless and had little power at court, where the influence of Catharine de'Medici was now paramount. In the same year her mother died, and she then returned to Scotland.

Brought up a Roman Catholic and used to the carefree life of the French court, she found the dominant Protestantism of Scotland and the austere manners of her subjects almost intolerable. Nevertheless, the first period of her reign was fairly successful; and she strove to placate the Protestants. The Protestants, however, were soon estranged by her unfortunate marriage with her cousin, Henry Stuart, Lord Darnley, and a Catholic, who on February 9, 1567, was blown up by gunpowder as the result of a treacherous plot he himself inspired. Three months later Mary married Earl of Bothwell, who was thought to have been involved in the murder of Darnley (Jackson, *Women Who Ruled,* p. 121).

From this time on a series of misfortunes struck the queen and a general revolutionary uprising took place. In the battle of Carberry Hill, Bothwell was defeated and fled, and Mary was confined in Lochleven Castle and compelled to abdicate. She escaped with her life and fled to England. Here she was immediately imprisoned, first at Carlisle, afterwards in various other places, and last in Fotheringay Castle. She was imprisoned for 18 year and finally beheaded by Elizabeth on October 25, 1586.

Mary II
Co-Regent with William III

Mary II was born at St. James Palace, Westminster, on April 30, 1662. She was the daughter of James II by Anne Hyde, his first wife.

Mary was married at the age of fifteen to William, Prince of Orange, on November 4, 1677. Two weeks after her marriage Mary and William sailed to The Hague and here they lived until February 12, 1689, when the couple returned to London.

The throne was declared vacant by the flight of James II and William and Mary were crowned as next heirs on April 11, 1689. Though Mary was declared joint possessor of the throne with her husband, yet the administration of the government was left entirely to him. She was not slighted in the least because this arrangement was according to Mary's own wishes. She is quoted as saying, "There is but one command which I wish him to obey, and that is 'Husband love your wives'. For myself, I shall follow the injunction, 'Wives, be obedient to your husbands in all things." (Jackson, *Women Who Ruled*, p. 119).

She kept the promise voluntarily made, and all her efforts were directed to promote her husband's happiness, and make him beloved by the English people. William had great confidence in Mary's abilities, and when, during his absence in Ireland, she was left the regent of the kingdom. She managed parties at home with much wisdom, and governed with discretion not inferior to his own.

The unfriendly terms, on which she lived with her sister, afterward Queen Anne, have often been alluded to as a blemish on Mary's character. But political jealousies, and the foolish attachment of Anne to overbearing favorites, may sufficiently account for this breach.

Aside from this alienation from her sister, Mary was in truth, an amiable and excellent queen, and by her example made industry and domestic virtue fashionable. She died of smallpox at Kensington in the year 1694.

Queen Anne
Queen of England

Anne, queen of Great Britain and Ireland, was born at St. James Palace, London, on February 6, 1665. She was the second daughter of James II of England by his first wife, Anne Hyde, the daughter of the famous Earl of Clarendon. When she was six years old, her mother died and her father soon after professed himself a member of the Church of Rome. Even so, his daughters were educated in the principles of the Church of England, to which Anne always retained an earnest if not a very enlightened loyalty.

Queen Anne was of middle size, and attractive, though not beautiful. She was virtuous, conscientious, and affectionate, more worthy of respect as a woman than of administration as a queen.

In 1683 Anne was married to Prince George of Denmark, a slothful yet good-natured man, who concerned himself little about public affairs, and had as little capacity for dealing with them.

At an early age she formed an intimacy with Sarah Jennings, afterwards the Duchess of Marlborough, who exercised an almost unbounded influence over her, both before and after her accession to the throne. She was the mother of seventeen children, all of whom died young and before she became queen.

In the revolution of 1688, Anne supported the cause of the Prince of Orange, but was afterwards implicated in intrigues for the restoration of her father. She succeeded William III who died March 8, 1702, at a time when the strife of parties was extremely violent. She pursued the foreign policy of the late king, which involved England in the long war of the Spanish succession as the ally of Austria and the enemy of France.

Among the important events of Anne's reign were a number of victories gained by the Duke of Marlborough over the armies of Louis XIV, and the union of England and Scotland in 1707. Her political principles, if she had any, were favorable to royal prerogative rather than constitutional liberty, and rendered her partial to the Tories.

Anne became gradually alienated from the Duchess of Marlborough, who as a Whig, and transferred her favoritism to Mrs. Masham, whose intrigues undermined the Whig party so effectively that the Tory statesmen, the Earl of Oxford and Lord Bolingbroke, came into power in 1710. The queen and these Tory ministers agreed in plans and schemes to secure the succession to her brother (Jackson, *Women Who Ruled*, p. 25). The treaty of Utrecht ended the European war, Lord Bolingbroke became prime minister in place of the Earl of Oxford, and the poor queen was kept in a state of constant unrest through the quarrels of her ministers. She died of a stroke on August 1, 1714 and was succeeded by George I.

Though not accredited to her, Queen Anne's reign was almost as famous in literature as the Augustan age of Rome, marked by such genius as Newton, Addison, Pope, Bolingbroke, Swift, DeFoe, and Arbuthnot.

Patricia R. Chadwick

Catherine I
Empress of Russia

Catherine I, Empress of Russia was originally a peasant's
daughter. Her original name was Martha Skavranska and her
parents lived at Ringen, a small village not far from Dorpt, on
Lake Vitcherve, in Livonia. The date of her birth was April
15, 1684. She was left an orphan when she was fifteen years
of age and from that time on she was brought up mainly by a
Lutheran pastor named Gluck, in Marienburg, Livonia.

In 1702 she married a Swedish horseman. The Russians,
however, took Marienburg in the same year, and Catharine
was made a prisoner. While a prisoner, she became the
mistress of Prince Menschikoff. It wasn't long before she
attracted the attention of Peter the Great, and won so much of
his affections that he married her in 1711. Some years prior to
this, however, she went over to the Greek Church, and took
the name of Catharina Alexievna.

When Peter the Great and his army seemed entirely in the
power of the Turkish army on the Pruth in 1711, Catherine,
according to the common account, used skillful bribery and
procured the deliverance of the Russians. From this time forth
she was received with great favor and was solemnly crowned
in 1712.

On the death of Peter the Great in 1725, she was acknowledged Empress and sole ruler of all the Russians. The first thing she did on her ascension was to cause every gallows to be taken down, and all instruments of torture to be destroyed. She instituted a new order of knighthood, and performed many actions worthy of a great mind.

She was much loved for her great humanity, but it wasn't long before she began to yield to the influence of a number of favorites and addicted herself to drunkenness. Her undisciplined lifestyle led to an early death on May 17, 1727. After she died, her daughter, Elizabeth, became empress in her place.

Patricia R. Chadwick

Queen Victoria
Beloved Queen

Queen Victoria is often considered England's most noble queen. If one were to list the events and progressive movements of Victoria's reign it would fill many pages. No similar period in the history of Europe has been filled with benefit to humanity.

Victoria was born in 1819 to Edward, Duke of Kent and Princess Louisa Victoria of Saxe-Coburg. Her father was the youngest son of George III and was sent to Hanover to be educated as a soldier. While there, Edward spent far too much money and incurred many debts. He returned to England without the permission of his father, and was then sent to Gibraltar and next to Canada, where he commanded the military forces of British America. Later he was made governor of Gibraltar and ruled it well.

When he was fifty years old he married Princess Louisa Victoria of Sax- Coburg, Queen Victoria's mother. Believing that his child would some day be sovereign of England, Edward desired that his child be born in his native land. He had to go into heavy debt to secure the funds to make this move, but the couple returned to England and made their home at Kensigton Palace, where Victoria was born.

Her father died eight months after her birth and the training of Victoria was left entirely up to her mother. Victoria received an excellent education and her mother was almost her constant companion. She was taught to speak three languages, English, German, and French and she also became familiar with Latin, Italian, and Greek as well. Victoria was also proficient in mathematics and the sciences.

Victoria became queen at the age of eighteen upon the death of her uncle William IV in 1837. She reigned until 1901, bestowing her name upon the time frame that she ruled: the Victorian Era (Bolton, *Famous Leaders,* p. 304). Two years after her coronation she married Prince Albert of Saxe-Coburg-Gotha, a nephew of her mothers. Albert soon became Victoria's chief advisor and he remained the focal point of Victoria's life, bearing him nine children. Theirs was an extremely happy union and their family was a model of home love and fidelity to all of England.

Albert died in 1861, leaving a desolate Victoria to live her life in a self-imposed seclusion for ten years. Thereafter she lived at Windsor or Balmoral, traveling abroad once a year, but making only a few public appearances in England.

Victoria died at Osborne House on the Isle of Wight, on January 22, 1901. She was as widely loved and honored in her life as she was in her death. The expressions of universal sorrow, which her death called forth from the entire civilized world, showed how widely she was respected as both a woman and a queen.

Patricia R. Chadwick

Empress Eugenie
Empress of France

Eugenie Marie de Montijo (pronounced yu zhay NEE ma REE they mawn TEE hoh) became empress of France as the wife of Napoleon III. The empress set standards for beauty and fashion in the French Court, having the best designers at her disposal. She also became noted for her extravagance.

Eugenie was the daughter of a Spanish officer and her mother was from Scotch Roman Catholic descent. A Spanish countess, she was born in Granada, Spain, in 1826.

Eugenie visited Paris the year before Louis Napoleon became emperor and was married to him in 1853, the year after he gained the throne. The city of Paris gave her a wedding gift of six hundred thousand francs, but at her request it was used to found a female college. With her husband she visited Queen Victoria and from that time on the Queen and Empress were close friends.

Politically influential, Eugenie favored the more traditional Roman Catholic party and she did whatever was in her power to delay a more liberal government in France. Eugenie served three times as regent of France, first when Napoleon was absent in Italy, again when he was making his Algerian tour, and finally, upon his departure to wage war against Germany. In fact, on the eve of the Franco-Prussian War, Eugenie urged warlike policy.

After the battle of Sedan, in which her husband was captured, she was urged to flee from Paris, as the streets were full of agitated people and the palace was being besieged by an infuriated mob. With the help of friends, Eugenie managed to get through the German lines, which guarded Paris, escaped to England, where the Emperor joined her upon his release (Adelman, *Famous Women,* p. 220). Napoleon and Eugenie were forced to live in exile from 1870 until her death in 1920.

Patricia R. Chadwick

Tsz Hsi An
Empress Dowager of China

One of the most powerful women in the nineteenth century was Tsze Hsi An, empress of China. She was likely the shrewdest woman of all of Asia during her era. She was considered by many at that time as "the only man in China" and probably exercised more power than any woman in her world. While queen Victoria had influence, Tsze Hsi An had power and it was power she fought for and won for herself (King, *Woman,* p. 462).

Tsze Hsi An's full name was Tszehi Toanyu Kangi Chaoyu Chuangcheng Shokung Chinhein Chungish. Though she was born in Peking, she was not actually Chinese, but a Manchu. You will recall that in 1644 the Manchu Tartars seized the throne of the Chinese Empire and kept it until 1912.

While looking at the life of Tszhe Hsi An., one must not over look another women, Tsze Hi, who became the principal wife of Prince Chun, the emperor's brother, while Tsze Hsi An, became the secondary wife of Emperor Hienfung. The emperor had no children, but his brother's wife gave birth to a son and Tsze Hi was raised to the rank of empress, though in reality still obliged to yield precedence to Tsze Hsi An. Tumultuous times came to China and the royal family had to flee to Tartary. In exile, the emperor died, leaving his frail throne to the son of Tsze Hi.

Tze Hsi An, now made herself felt in the game of royalty. By an unwritten law of China, she should have killed herself as a mark of respect for being childless. But she ignored that law and followed another law, which required the children of inferior wives to regard the chief wife as their mother. Tsze Hsi An thus found a way not to die and the boy came under the joint control of the two matrons.

In due time, the prince was proclaimed emperor and the two mothers as regents. Having arrived at the proper age, he assumed the reins of government and the ladies retired to the background. In 1874, the new emperor died of small pox, and the two dowagers once again came forward.

Being women, they could not rule in their own right, so they looked for a child to adopt. They found a nephew of Tsze Hi, who was three years old. That child became Emperor Kuangsii. When Kuangsii was about eight years old, Tsze Hi died, and Tsze Hsi An was left as sole dowager, master of the child and the empire. The young prince became of age in 1889 and was crowned emperor, but he was little more than a puppet in the hands of Tsze Hsi An.

At the beginning of the war with Japan, Tsze Hsi An stepped in and sent her old favorite Li Hung Chang to Japan to make peace. Later, when the emperor was starting out on a series of reforms by the adoption of Western ideas, she assumed control of the affairs and in one sweep all the decrees of the emperor were annulled and six leaders of the reform party were executed. Among them was Chang Yin Yuan, the president of the Board of Revenue and former ambassador to the United States.

After this, it was announced that Emperor Kuangsii had committed suicide, which was the Chinese form of execution. This announcement proved to be false. Kuangsii was kept alive by Tsze Hsi An as a puppet emperor so that she could continue to rule China with her iron hand until her death in 1908.

Tsze His An's life was one of extremes, having been criticized much by her enemies, and wildly praised by her admirers. It cannot be disputed, however, that she was a great ruler and that she had a profound influence on world history.

6

Sarah Jane Lippincott
The Legendary "Grace Greenwood"

Charlotte Yonge
Novelist and Historian

Louisa May Alcott
Author of Little Women

Jenny Lind
"The Swedish Nightingale"

Clara Louise Kellog
Opera Singer

Adelina Maria Patti
Opera Singer

Harriet Hosmer
Sculptor

Vinnie Ream Hoxie
Sculptor

Sarah Siddons
Actress

Sarah Jane Lippincott
The Legendary "Grace Greenwood"

Sarah Jane Lippincott was a nineteenth century journalist, author, and philanthropist who is better known by her pen name of "Grace Greenwood". In fact, she chose the name because she thought it better fit her tastes and talents.

Sarah was born in Pompey, New York as Sarah Jane Clarke. As a child she loved nature and found much delight in the romping around in the fields and forests of her little town. She was quite athletic and daring. In fact, she outdid many of the boys of her town in daring deeds. Another great love of hers was to ride horses. And in this she preferred to ride bareback.

As a young girl Sarah attended school in Rochester, N.Y., and while she was a good student, she cared little for mathematics and the sciences. She could, however, write verses and sketches with so much skill that publishers sought to publish her work before she was even fourteen years old. They thought her writings fresh and racy.

Sarah had her own style of writing. No one could be like her and she could not be like anyone else. She was simply and intensely herself. Sarah wrote several titles under her pseudonym, including *Greenwood Leaves, History of My Pets, Poems, Recollections of My Childhood, Haps and*

Mishaps of a Tour in Europe, Forest Tragedy and Other Tales, Stories of Many Lands, History for Children, Victoria Queen of England. Her book on Queen Victoria was published simultaneously in London and New York. She also wrote for several periodicals either as a contributor or an editor and delivered many notable lectures and speeches.

In 1853, when Sarah was thirty years old, she married Leander K. Lippincott of Philadelphia. During the Civil War, Sarah took up the cause of the sick and injured soldiers. She rendered excellent service on their behalf by lecturing for the fairs of the Sanitary Commission, which were instituted by Mary A. Livermore to raise funds to meet the needs of the soldiers. Sarah also lectured to the soldiers in camp, and President Lincoln dubbed her "Grace Greenwood, the patriot".

Charlotte Yonge
English Novelist and Historian

Charlotte Yonge has been a most prolific writer, having published over one hundred and twenty-five volumes of fiction and a large number of national histories for younger readers.   Her work included schoolbooks, religious texts, historical novels, and tales of everyday life.   She was an ardent supporter of high-church views, which is apparent in all her works.   Although she wrote profusely, she always maintained high quality in all her work

While many authors achieve fame after their . death, Charlotte achieved great success during her lifetime. During her lifetime she was very popular and her books were read and admired by other great authors such as Louisa May Alcott, Lord Tennyson, Lewis Carroll, and many others. She gained a wide circle of readers by her book *The Heir of Redclyffe*, which appeared in 1853. A large part of the early profits from this book were used to outfit the missionary schooner, *Southern Cross* for Bishop Selwyn. She used the part of the profits from her book *Daisy Chain* to help build a missionary college in New Zealand. She also wrote many works of fiction including, *Lances of Lynwood, Scenes from the Life of a Spinster*, and *Clever Woman of the Family*.

Patricia R. Chadwick

Charlotte's historical works included Greece, Rome, France, Germany, England, and the United States. She also wrote such books as *History of Christian Names and Their Derivation* and *Story of English Missionary Workers.* Several of her histories were rewritten so that they could be read and enjoyed by the small children, such as *Aunt Charlotte's Roman History for the Little Ones.*

Since most of Yonge's fiction work reflected everyday life during the Victorian era, we see in them the introduction of the education of women and their status in the community. Charlotte was homeschooled by her parents and remained a staunch supporter of educating women at home throughout her career. Even though there was a marked increase of women receiving a high school education and an increasing number of women's colleges being founded, Charlotte always felt that the best education for young women was Home Education.

Louisa May Alcott
Author of "Little Women"

Louisa May Alcott was born in Germantown, Pennsylvania on November 29,1832. During her childhood the family moved to Concord, Massachusetts. Her father was the noted A. Bronson Alcott, the "Sage of Concord", and intimate friend of Ralph Waldo Emerson. While he had a great mind, he was an idealist and didn't regularly provide for his families necessities. Her mother, Abigail May was of old-line Boston stock, and was of prominent lineage. She was a woman of incredible stamina, wisdom, and love. She was a patient woman, as was much needed being married to an abstracted idealist   It was Abigail Alcott who kept the family together, encouraging the failing husband in his moments of depression, and making ends meet by accepting menial work. She became an inspiration and role model to the young Louisa. While much of her youth was lived in poverty, Louisa's early surroundings were of a highly intellectual and literary character, and she naturally took to writing while she was very young.

Due to the family's low income and the burdens of her mother, Louisa felt compelled to become a wage earner to help support the family, so she taught school, served as a governess, worked as a domestic servant, traveling companion, and took in work as a seamstress. She was later to use these experiences in her novels.

Becoming weary of menial tasks, she began to write sensational stories, such as thrillers, for the local papers, which were financially lucrative. At this time she wrote mostly anonymously or using a pseudonym. But her conscience was not easy in this matter, and she abandoned the writing of such tales. Instead, she began writing from her experiences and her confidence began to grow.

In 1865, Louisa became the companion to an invalid lady and traveled to Europe. This trip supplied her with material for ensuing travel pieces. Upon her return, she was again compelled to earn a wage, due to her families debts and needs, so she continued her writing. In 1867 she turned to the juvenile field and accepted the editorship of Merry's Museum, a girls' magazine. With accepting this job, she moved to Boston.

The following year, she was approached by the Roberts Brothers publishing firm to write a novel for adolescent girls along the lines of those for boys written by Oliver Optic. With her family's encouragement, Louisa set to work on such a novel. She had keen powers of observation and sensitivity to adolescence that proved to be a winning combination. She used her personal experiences and faith in God to form the plot of her book and the cast of characters for her novel came from her own family.

While her published works numbered more than 270 items, many of which were written for young girls, Louisa May is best known for the novel, *Little Women*, which was written in its entirety in only two six week periods. This story gives to us a charming and straightforward picture of nineteenth-century life, as seen through the eyes of an adolescent girl of the day. Miss Alcott is associated in the minds of many as Jo March, the tomboy heroine of Little Women.

Little Women was an immediate success. Letters poured in from thousands of young ladies who were touched by the book and especially the character of Jo March. It reached a sale of 87,000 in three years. Louisa followed up this work with *An Old Fashioned Girl* and *Little Men*. Other works that followed were *Aunt Jo's Scrap Bag*, in six volumes, *Modern Mephistopheles, Proverb Stories, Spinning Wheel Stories, Jo's Boys*, and *A Garland for Girls*. She also wrote *Hospital Sketches*, which was her last record of her own experiences in ministering to the sick and wounded.

Miss Alcott had ambition and ability for a high grade of literary work. While she could have continued pursuing a lucrative career in sensational writing, following her conscience rewarded her. She found true success as a writer of children's stories, thus becoming a "moral guardian" to young girls the world over.

Patricia R. Chadwick

Jenny Lind
"Swedish Nightingale"

Jenny Lind was born in Stockholm, Sweden, in 1821, the daughter of a language teacher. She is said to have been able to repeat a song that she had heard but once at the age of three. At ten years of age she sang children parts on the Stockholm stage. After turning 12 years of age, her upper notes lost their sweetness, and for four years she did not do much singing. Her love for music continued and these years were devoted to the study of instrumental music and composition.

At the end of this period her voice had recovered its power and purity and for a year and a half she was the star of the Stockholm opera. Next, she gave a series of concerts to obtain the means to go to Paris for further study, but the French teacher did not appreciate her powers and Jenny returned to her native city.

When she was twenty-three years old, Jenny went to Dresden and when Queen Victoria visited that city the following year, she sang at the festivals held in the queen's honor. This opened the way to astonishing success in other German cities. In 1847 she went to London and was enthusiastically received. Here she sang for the first time in concert.

Because of the influence of P.T. Barnum, Jenny Lind visited America in 1850. Because of his great influence and his power as an advertiser he roused the wildest enthusiasm. Tickets sold for fabulous prices in New York. But she did not disappoint the wildest expectation.

She subsequently married Mr. Otto Goldschmidt of Boston, a musician and conductor. After her marriage, she appeared on the stage only at intervals and usually at concerts given for charitable causes. She was deeply interested in these charitable causes and we can easily add to her title of singer that of philanthropist.

Her later years were spent in London where she died in 1886. Her life and songs are a sweet memory.

Patricia R. Chadwick

Clara Louise Kellog
American Opera Singer

Clara Louise Kellogg was a nineteenth century female vocalist. Though her career was fraught with numerous failures, she was determined to become a professional singer. She continued to cultivate her voice until she was considered one of the finest singers in American. She also was the first American singer to win recognition in Europe.

Clara Louise Kellogg was born in 1842 at Sumpterville, South Carolina, but her childhood was spent in the North. Both of her parents were of considerable note, her father being inventor George Kellog, and her mother being an excellent musician. She was evidently born a singer, for at nine months old she could hum a tune correctly.

When she was fourteen years old, Clara's parents move the family to New York for Clara to begin a thorough course of musical studies. A professional career was in the minds of both parents from the start and all her training had that end in view.

Sarah studied both the French and Italian methods of singing and made a special study of Marguerite in Gounod's *Faust,* and in that no one has ever equaled her. Beriloz was in the United States at the time and heard her. He was astonished at the skill with which se interpreted the subtler shadings of the poet, which he believed were beyond the reach of lyric art.

Upon appearing in Her Majesty's Theater in London, as Marguerite, she won a brilliant victory. She also sang in the Handel Festival held in the great Crystal Palace, a great honor for an American.

When she returned to America, the public was ready to receive her and she was met by crowds everywhere she performed. In one winter she sang over one hundred and fifty nights. After some years she accepted an engagement in Austria, where she sang in Italian with a German opera company. She even journeyed to Russia and sang in St. Petersburg.

Clara had a good heart and was always offered help to struggling artists. She was quite wealthy by the end of her career and spent much of it on philanthropic enterprises.

Patricia R. Chadwick

Adelina Maria Patti
Opera Singer

Adelina Maria Patti was considered one of the greatest female vocalists of her time. Her pure, sweet soprano voice and radiant technique made fast fans of all who heard her. Her voice was considered small, but was noted for its wide range, evenness of production, and purity of quality. Besides her voice of exceptional beauty, range, and flexibility, she possessed rare powers as an actress. Adelina achieved great success in comedy and is often remembered for her role in Rossini's *The Barber of Seville*.

Born on February 19, 1843, Adelina Juana Maria Patti was the daughter of opera singers. Her father, Salvatore Patti, was a tenor, and her mother; Caterina Chiesa Barilli-Patti was a soprano. At the birth of Adelina, her mother lost her voice. This was such a tragedy to the family that they moved from Madrid, Spain, Adenlia's birthplace, to America.

When she was four years old, Adelina showed remarkable musical talent and took piano lessons from her sister, Carlotta, and vocal lessons from her stepbrother, Barili and her brother-in-law Strakosch, who had great talent as a singer and had won considerable respect in the music world. These advantages, coupled with her inherited musical taste and ability, helped Adelina achieve the most and long continued training.

At the age of nine, Adelina appeared in concert with Strakosch and was an instant success. A series of concerts followed and Adelina received a share of the profits, giving her $10,000. In this series Strakosch and Ole Bull were instrumentalists. She was the child prima donna.

After several years of success in America, South America, and the West Indies, she made her operatic debut as Lucia in Gaetano Donizetti's *Lucia di Lammermoor* at the New York Academy of Music. After this she went to Europe with Strakosch, but the London manager would not even give her an opportunity to sing. As they were about to return to America, the manager of the Covent Garden Theater gave her permission to sing three times, but without pay. She made her first appearance in Bellini's *Sonnambula* and was adored by the public. Her triumph immediate, Adelina's career was to the people of London like a blazing meteor. After this debut, the way was opened to her in France, Germany, Italy, Spain, and Russia. When she wasn't touring, Adelina was a regular performer at Covent Gardens, singing many roles in the operas of Gioacchino Rossini, Bellini, Giacomo Meyerbeer, Charles Bounod, and in several of the early operas of Giuseppe Verdi. In fact, Verdi at one time declared her "the greatest singer" he had ever heard.

In 1868, Adelina married Marquis de Caux in London. The marriage only lasted ten years and then the couple divorced. In 1886 Adelina married Signor Nicolini, a fellow opera singer.

Adelina was also a fine actress. Though to small of stature to personate the great characters of the highest style of tragic opera, she did excel in parts requiring archness and the art of flirting. She also met with success in roles of passion and sentiment, as in Donizetti's *Lucia* or Gounod's *Marguerite.*

Adelina's farewell performance occurred at the Royal Albert Hall, London, in December 1906, though she continued to make guest appearances occasionally. She retired to Craig-y Nos Castle, which was her estate in Brecknockshire, Wales, until her death on September 27, 1919.

Hariett Hosmer
American Sculptor

Harriet Hosmer has brought honor to both her country and her sex by her brilliant work as a sculptor. She proved that Americans can be sculptors and that a woman can handle a chisel as well as palette and brush.

Harriet Hosmer was born in Watertown, Massachusetts. She enjoyed a very active childhood with much physical exercise. Since her mother and older sister died of tuberculosis, her physician father encouraged her to spend much time outdoors in the open air. Harriet soon became an all around athlete, participating in hunting, fishing, rowing, and horseback riding. In the fields and forests she gained a thorough knowledge of animal life, and when while she was but a child she began to model dogs, horses, and other animals in a clay pit near her home. The physical strength that she acquired in her childhood would enable her afterward to wield the four-pound mallet for eight or ten hours per day that was required of a sculptor.

While her studies were of secondary importance, she was still given a good education. Harriet was sent to a progressive school that fostered independence and provided her with creative women role models. She soon found that sculpting was her forte and she went to St. Louis to study anatomy.

Next she went to Rome and became the pupil of the famous sculptor, John Gibson, where she attracted the patronage of affluent tourists. For her work, *The Sleeping Faun*, she received $5,000. Harriet was not the only female sculptor in Rome at this time, but became one of a group of American women sculptors dubbed the *White Marmorean Flock*. She also joined herself to a large circle of international artists and writers and became a great success. Some of her most famous works are *Zenobia in Chains* and *Queen of Palmyra.*

Vinnie Ream Hoxie
Sculptor

Vinnie Ream Hoxie was an American Sculptor. She enjoys the distinction of being the first woman to receive an order from the United States government for a statue.

Vinnie Ream Hoxie was born one of three children in Madison, Wisconsin on September 25, 1846. Her parents were Robert Lee Ream and Lavinia McDonald Ream. Vinnie's family moved around a lot as she grew up. When she was ten, her family moved to western Missouri where she attended the academy section of Christian College in Columbia, Missouri. She showed a talent for music and art. When the Civil War began, the family was now in Fort Smith, Arkansas where her father worked in Real Estate. At this time they wanted to move to Washington, D.C. The family managed to skirt the Confederate Troops in order to get there and upon settling in Washington, Robert was given a government job and Vinnie became a clerk in the Post Office Department. It was here that Vinnie was to spend most of her life.

When she was living in Washington, Vinnie discovered her own taste and talent for art and devoted her energies to the arts, with special emphasis on sculpture.   In 1863 she visited the studio of sculptor Clark Mills and there decided to try her hand at sculpting. She found she had a talent for it and Mr. Mills took her on as a student because he was so impressed with her work. Before long she was sculpting busts of important men in Washington such as Congressmen, Senators, and others of prominence. Her models included such men as General Grant, John Sherman, and Thaddeus Stevens. She also produced *The Indian Girl*, which was a full-length figure cast in bronze, and *Miriam* which was done in marble and was of her most noted creations.

But one of the crowning honors of her career was the opportunity to produce a statue of Abraham Lincoln, which she executed in bronze, to be placed in the Capitol. In 1864, some friends of hers had arranged with President Lincoln for him to pose for Vinnie in order that she might make a bust of him. At first he refused, but relented upon hearing that Vinnie was a poor girl, struggling to make her own way in the world. He gave her half-hour sittings over five months and the bust she created was well received. In 1866, Congress awarded her a $10,000 contract to do a full-size marble statue of Lincoln to stand in the Capitol rotunda. She was the first woman to receive such a federal commission.

After she finished the model, Vinnie took it to Italy to be transferred to marble. Her parents accompanied her and together they lived in Rome for three years. While there, George P.A. Healy and Caleb Bingham painted Vinnie and Gustave Dore gave her a one of his own paintings and inscribed it personally.

In 1871 the finished statue of President Lincoln was unveiled. It was an awesome production and it was positively received by Washington society. The statue was so well liked that in 1875 Vinnie receive another federal commission for 420,000 to sculpt a bronze statue of Admiral David G. Farragut, a naval hero. While she was working on the model for this statue, Vinnie married Lieutenant Richard Leveridge Hoxie. At the request of her husband, Vinnie gave up sculpting for money, but continued to sculpt for love.

Patricia R. Chadwick

Sarah Siddons
Actress

Sarah Siddons is thought by many to have been the greatest English tragic actress of her time. She is celebrated for such Shakespearean roles as Desdemona in *Othello* and Volumnia in *Coriolanus*, and she was unequaled as Lady Macbeth. As an actress Sarah Siddons stands unapproached in every line of tragedy. Her passion, her rage, her despair, her sufferings, her grief, all being perfect in expression and convincing in naturalness.

Sarah Siddons was born in Brecon, Breckonshire, Wales on July 5, 1755, the eldest child of Roger and Sarah Kemble. Roger Kemble was a respectable manager of a small traveling theatrical company, whose circuit was the midland and westerns parts of England. From her earliest childhood she was a member of her father's troupe, and in a playbill, dated February 12, 1767, her name appears in the production of *Charles the First*, assigned to the character of the Princess Elizabeth. Even though she was accustomed to appearing on stage as a child, Mrs. Kremble took special care to send Sarah to schools in the towns where the company played, so she received a particularly good education.

As a young woman of seventeen, Sarah became infatuated with William Siddons, a member of her father's theatrical company. While he was a handsome man, he was somewhat of a dull actor. Her parents did not approve of the romance, but she married to him on November 26, 1773. Shortly afterwards she was recommended to Garrick by the Earl of Ailesbury and the result was an engagement at Drury Lane, where she made her first appearance in the character of Portia. At the end of the season she was let go and for the next six years she toured in the country, becoming well known as the queen of tragedy on the English Stage. Her reputation grew exceedingly fast and she was invited to return to Drury Lane. She accepted the offer and made her reappearance as Isabella in *The Fatal Marriage*. She met with immediate success and was from this time to her retirement the unquestioned queen of the stage. She reigned the queen at Drury Lane until 1803 when she and her brother went to Covent Garden. In 1783 she was appointed to teach oratory to the royal children.

Sarah played many of the great roles of tragedy during her career. Among her greatest roles were Isabella Belvidera in *Vanice Preserv'd*, Jane Shore in *The Tragedy of Jane Shore*, Katharine in *Henry VIII*, Constance in *King John*, Zara in *The Mourning Bride*, and Volumnia in *Coriolanus*, but it was Lady Macbeth that was her most successful role. It is said that her success was due to her complete concentration upon the characters that she played. She identified herself with appeared oblivious to all around her.

Sarah retired from the regular stage on June 29, 1812, with a farewell performance as Lady Macbeth. After her retirement from the stage, she gave occasional public readings, from Shakespeare and Milton. Sarah Siddons died on June 8, 1831.

7

Women of Faith

Martha and Mary
Bethany Sisters

Dorcas
Queen of the Needle

Priscilla
Missionary Tentmaker

Phoebe
Deaconess of Cenchrea

Lydia
The First Christian Convert in Europe

Catherine of Sienna
Saint and Literary Celebrity

Margaret Beufort
Mother of Henry VII of England

Selina Hastings
Patroness of Revival

Amy Carmichael
Founder of Dohnavur Fellowship

Catherine Booth
Co-founder of the Salvation Army

Pundita Ramabai Sarvesvati
Bible Translator

Fanny Crosby
Hymn Writer and Poet

Emeline Dryer
Christian Educator

Patricia R. Chadwick

Susannah Spurgeon
Founder of the Book Fund

Joni Eareckson Tada]
Founder of Joni & Friends Ministry

Anne Graham Lotz
Bible Teacher/Conference Speaker

Martha and Mary
Bethany Sisters

Mary and Martha were two sisters, who were very different, but each was the compliment of the other and both were the friends of Jesus. They opened their home to Jesus, both helping to make their home in Bethany a restful place to which He could come from the murderous plottings of the priests and Pharisees.

Martha was probably the elder of the two and she was a vigorous, bustling homemaker. From the narrative found in the Luke 10, it is obvious that Martha was over-careful about a multitude of unimportant details of the household. She was undoubtedly proud of her perfectly ordered home, but she had almost become a slave to her house.

Mary, on the other hand, appears to have more of a hunger for spiritual things. When Christ came to their home she took the opportunity, not to entertain Him, but to learn from Him.

While Martha was angry with Mary for leaving all the work to her during Jesus' visit, Jesus commended Mary and told Martha that she was unnecessarily burdening herself with over-carefulness and much serving. Jesus did honor Martha's zeal and she shared equally in Jesus' affection.

We meet Martha and Mary again in the Gospel of John,

chapter 11, when bereavement has come to the family. Their brother, Lazarus, the beloved friend of Jesus, has died. The girls had sent word to Jesus of his illness, but by the time he arrives in Bethany, Lazarus is dead. Martha is the first to meet Him and hear the wonderful word of comfort, "I am the Resurrection and the Life." Their brother is restored to them, the broken circle being made whole.

Shortly before the death of Christ, we find Him again in Bethany (John 12). He is in the house of Simon the leper, where a banquet is being held in His honor. Martha is found serving, once again, but this time with a different attitude. She willingly serves at the table, lovingly ministering to the physical comfort of the guest, without resentment. Mary too is here, and she brings in an alabaster box of ointment and anoints the head and feet of Jesus in a manner fit for royalty. Thus the two sisters, each in their own way, shows their devotion to Christ.

Dorcas
Queen of the Needle

Dorcas stands out in the Bible as a woman of good works and charitable deeds. While the record of her in the Christian Scripture is limited to a few verses in the ninth chapter of Acts, her name, even today, stands for the charitable use of the needle. Her example has inspired women throughout history to take upon themselves the needs of the poor.

Dorcas lived during the first century A.D. She made her home in Joppa and was associated with a little band of Christians, most of who were poor. Dorcas, herself, appears to be a wealthy woman, for her charitable deeds were numerous.

While the Bible gives us only glimpses of her benevolent works and her witness for Christ in the book of Acts, her influence is felt even today. She is evidently a Christian, being called "a certain disciple". There was a church in Joppa that was established at an early date by Phillip the evangelist. From it's very beginning, the church in Joppa was known as a center of enthusiastic evangelism with a well-organized benevolent work. It is possible that Dorcas came to Christ in this church and from there was taught the concept of service to mankind.

Dorcas proved herself to be a real "doer" of the Word of God, not just a mere "hearer". What is significant about the account of her life is that Dorcas not only thought up ways of relieving the needy, but she also carried out her plans. She knew what she could do and she DID it! Among her charitable deeds were making clothes for widows and the needy of her church community with her own hands. She was not only willing to give money to a cause, but she was willing to invest herself in the works of kindness.

While Dorcas is noted for her charitable deeds, she is also well known for her life being miraculously restored to her. According to the Bible, Dorcas died and was brought back to life at the hands of the Apostle Peter. When she died, Dorcas left the church at Joppa grief-stricken. Leaders of the congregation called for the Apostle Peter, who was visiting a neighboring city. Peter was renowned for his supernatural power and the church doubtless hoped that he might be able to restore Dorcas to them. When Peter came to the place that she lay, he found that the widows that Dorcas had helped had laid her out and prepared an eloquent eulogy on the life and character of their greatly loved patroness by displaying some of the many coats and garments which she had made for them. There were aged widows whose hands were too feeble to sew and too poor to pay others for their work. They showed the warm garments Dorcas had made them to protect them from the cold winds. And there were younger widows whose little children had been clothed by Dorcas. They yearned for the Apostle Peter to bring her back.

The scene apparently touched Peter's emotions. He sent them all out of the room and then he kneeled down and prayed. When he was sure that God was going to grant his request, Peter spoke the word of power and authority and raised Dorcas from the dead. He then presented her alive to congregation at Joppa.

While Dorcas was greatly loved and respected by the church at Joppa, apparently she wasn't conscious of the affect her work was having on people. She didn't strive to be a leader, but was content to stay in her own home and do all she could to serve God in her sphere of influence. Yet, because of her faithful service, she did indeed become a leader in philanthropic causes. Many women throughout history have formed "Dorcas Societies", holding humanitarian ideals and engaging in various relief activities. To women throughout the ages, Dorcas has been a fine example benevolence.

Patricia R. Chadwick

Priscilla
Missionary Tentmaker

Aquilla and Priscilla, a noble Christian couple, had been driven from Rome by the decree of Claudius Caesar. A large Jewish colony dwelt at Rome in a crowded quarter on the banks of the Tiber. A Roman historian, Suetonius, tells us that Claudius banished the Jews from Rome because of the constant disturbances of certain Jews that followed Christ. During the early decades of Christianity, the Romans did not distinguish between Jews and Christians. Some Jews who were converted at Jerusalem on the day of Pentecost had no doubt introduced Christianity into Rome. These Christians were undoubtedly persecuted by their fellow Jews, causing disturbances in the capital city. It was because of these disturbances that the whole Jewish colony was banished.

Aquilla and Priscilla were already Christians when they met the Apostle Paul. They had settled in Corinth where they were in the business of tent making. Upon his entrance to the city of Corinth, Paul met this couple and made his home with them. A three-fold tie attached them: they were Jews by birth, Christians by profession, and tentmakers by trade. While Paul was ministering in Corinth, he worked with his friends at their trade.

He was so successful in his missionary work that at the end of a year and a half the Jews raised such a persecution that all three were driven from the city to Ephesus, where Paul met some friends and sailed to Syria.

Sometime after Paul's departure, a learned and eloquent Jewish man of Alexandria came to Ephesus. His name was Apollos. Apollos had heard of and accepted the Christian religion and was working enthusiastically among his own people. When Aquilla and Priscilla heard him preach they were impressed by his ability and zeal, but they came to realize that he was not fully educated in Christian teaching. They invited him to their home and offered to teach him more fully the truth of Christianity. Priscilla and Aquilla became his teachers, and it is actually Priscilla who is given more honor in this matter, which is shown by her name being placed before that of her husband in the written record (Acts 18).

A few years later the couple evidently returned to Rome, for Paul in his letter to the Romans sends them greetings (Romans 16:4). In this single verse we learn that Paul remembered them as his "helpers" in the gospel work, no doubt thinking of the days in Corinth. Again, he says they had saved his life at the risk of their own. And, lastly, he speaks of "the church, which is in their house." Their home had become the meeting place of the Christians in Rome at a time when it was neither possible nor safe for them to have a special house of worship.

Patricia R. Chadwick

Phoebe
Deaconess of Cenchrea

There comes a time in everyone's life that we need help. The Apostle Paul was no different. The book of 2 Corinthians, chapter 11 lists the many trials he faced. But in the face of those trials, God gave Paul a helper. Her name was Phoebe, a woman from Cenchrea.

Cenchrea was the seaport of Corinth. The Apostle Paul had established a Christian church here. While working in Corinth he wrote his famous letter to the Romans and sent it by the hand of Phoebe. In Romans, chapter 16, her name stands at the head of a long list of noble workers.

Phoebe is called a "servant" of the church, but the word in the original language is "diakonos" from which we get our word deacon. So, while she is called a "servant" of the church, it truly should be translated a "deacon" of the church. The use of this term shows us that it was likely that Phoebe had an official position in the church at Corinth.

It appears that Phoebe was also a business woman, having had affairs of her own to attend to in Rome, for Paul urges the Christians at Rome to be of any possible assistance to her. Paul pays her high tribute by saying she has been of great help to many people, including himself.

Phoebe used both her financial means and her own person to minister to the sick and distressed of her city. She was a useful worker and co-laborer with the Apostle Paul, and is noted in the Bible for her faithful service.

Patricia R. Chadwick

Lydia
First European Convert to Christianity

Her native place was Thyatira on the borders of Lydia in Asia Minor. Her city was celebrated in ancient times for its purple dyes and fabrics. Among the ruins of the city has been found an inscription relating to the "Guild of Dyers", showing the accuracy in unimportant details of this Scripture narrative.

She may have been known by a different name at home, but among strangers she was known as Lydia or the Lydian. She was a businesswoman, dealing in colored material, or more likely goods already died. The color purple was highly prized among the ancients and Lydia was a merchant that sold purple cloth. Given the circumstances revealed in the Bible, it's safe to assume she was a very successful entrepreneur.

Lydia had settled in the city of Philippi, which was a miniature Rome. Here she carried on her trade, surrounded by her household that seems to have included many servants. She was not a Jewess by birth, but she is noted as having been a "worshiper of God" (Acts 16:14). She had obviously come to a knowledge of the one, true God and as a result, she became a devout follower.

Philippi was the scene of the first labors of Paul in Europe. One Sabbath day he found a company of Jews worshiping outside the city, near a river. He preached to them and Lydia became a Christian. She at once urged the missionaries to make her house their home. Paul, not liking to be dependent on anyone, hesitated, but finally accepted her hospitality.

It is apparent that the home of Lydia soon became a meeting place for Christians. Considering the trials that Paul had endured, he must have found much comfort being cared for in this home. After being jailed for freeing a slave girl from demon possession, Paul and Silas were asked to leave the city. A farewell gathering was held at Lydia's home and we may suppose that the converted Philippian jailer was one of the company!

Paul departed to carry the gospel message to other cities of Europe, yet he held the church in Philippi close to his heart. The church that began in the home of Lydia, worshiper of God, became perhaps the most loved body of believers to the Apostle Paul and he was their beloved apostle. Though not rich in material wealth, they supported Paul in his missionary work whenever possible, and it was to the church at Philippi that Paul wrote his most loving epistle from the prison in Rome.

Patricia R. Chadwick

Catherine of Siena
Saint and Literary Celebrity

Catherine of Siena is considered a Catholic Saint who lived in Siena, Italy. Early in life she devoted herself to an austere life. The monks tell us that she became a nun of the Dominican order at a young age and that she saw numerous visions and wrought many miracles while quite young.

Catherine Benicasa was born to a lower-middle-class family that was politically active family in Siena. When she was fifteen, she refused her parents' plans for her to marry and three years later she received the habit of the Dominican Third Order women's group, which were lay people affiliated with the order. She stayed in the home of her parents until she was twenty-one, living in seclusion and practicing bodily austerities. It was during this time that she learned to read.

She soon became celebrated for her recluse life, revelations, and miraculous powers of conversion. But one of her visionary experiences led her out into the community to serve others. For six years she worked with the poor and the sick, especially victims of the plague and famine in and around Siena. Her reputation for holiness caused her to have a following of would-be disciples. The growth of this following made her well known outside her own city.

In 1374, she attended the Dominican general chapter that was held in Florence, which marked the beginning of her involvement in politics. Her influence was so great that she reconciled Pope Gregory XI to the people of Avignon, in 1376, after he had excommunicated them; and in 1377 she prevailed upon him to reestablish the pontifical seat at Rome, seventy years after Clement V had removed it to France. While even Petrarch and Dante could not persuade the Pope to return to Rome, Catherine was successful. This moved the center of Europe back again to its old place in Rome after the princes of the Church and the greatest men of Italy had attempted it in vain.

Many legends surround the person of Catherine of Siena. One such legend states that in revenge for the defeat of a company of heathen philosophers with whom she had been compelled to dispute, Catherine was bound to a wheel with spikes, in such a way that every turn of the machine would cause the spikes to pierce her body. According to legend, the cords were miraculously broken, and the malice of her enemies foiled. Consequently St. Catherine is always represented with a wheel and the extreme popularity of this saint is indicated by the fact that a wheel of a certain construction and appearance is often called the Catherine wheel (King, *Woman*, p. 210).

Her literary works consisted of letters, poems, and devotional pieces. The letters are by far the most interesting and valuable of her works. Catherine of Siena died on April 30, 1380 in Rome.

Patricia R. Chadwick

Margaret Beufort
Mother of King Henry VII of England

Margaret Beaufort was born at Bletshoe in Bedfordshire in 1441 the only daughter and heiress of John Beuufort, the first Duke of Somerset, grandson to John of Gaunt, Duke of Lancaster and great-grandson of Edward III. Her mother was Margaret Beauchamp. Her father died when she was only three years old and she was brought up by her mother with the greatest care and devotion. While she was very young she was married to Edmund Tudor, Earl of Richmond, by whom she had a son named Henry who was to become Henry VII, king of England.

Edmund died soon after the birth of their son, leaving Margaret a young widow with a fifteen week old baby to care for. In 1459 Margaret married Lord Henry Stafford. Lord Henry was her cousin on both her father and mother's side, who traced his roots to Henry III. They were married for 23 years, but had no children. Her third husband was the Earl of Derby who died in 1504.

Lady Beufort was a devout woman and a model of piety and devotion. She was well known for her benevolence and acts of charity, though her life was slightly tinged with asceticism. She rose at five in the morning and from that hour until around ten o'clock in the morning she spent her time in prayer and meditation. In her house she kept constantly twelve poor people, whom she provided with food and clothing. She also gave of her self to those less fortunate. Although she was the mother of the king, Margaret was often found dressing the wounds of the lowest beggars and relieving them by her medicinal skills.

Besides her private acts of charity and her gifts to religious houses, she was a generous patron of learning, donating much money for its encouragement. She established Readerships in the Divinity at Oxford and Cambridge. Two public lectures in divinity were instituted by Lady Beufort, one at both colleges, and those generous efforts were only surpassed by her liberality to God's House at Cambridge, which was reestablished as Christ's College with her funding. She also provided the funds for the founding of St. John's College. She was a mother to the students of both universities and a patroness to all the learned men of England.

Historians agree that while applauding her many outstanding qualities and virtues, there are only a few things to criticize about her life, which were really only errors of the age in which she lived. Catholics not only see the important part she played in the civil land political history of her time, but they also perceive her life was a high example of the Christian life. Her firm and robust faith bore its natural and wholesome fruits in deeds of benevolence. Margaret Beaufort died in 1509.

Patricia R. Chadwick

Selina Hasting
Patroness of Revival

During a time when women didn't have many opportunities to publicly serve the Lord, Selina Hastings shines forth as an example of how God can accomplish His work by using a woman who is totally devoted to Him. While many people have at least some knowledge of the great "Methodist Revival" that took place under the Wesley's and George Whitefield in 18th century England, not many are aware that the fires of revival were spread due, in part, to the diligent efforts and financial backing of one woman: Selina Hastings, Countess of Huntingdon.

Selina was born in England in 1707, the daughter of Washington Shirley, Earl of Ferrars. She lived her young life among the aristocracy and at age 21 she was married to Theophilus Hastings, Earl of Huntingdon. Though she was raised to fear God, it wasn't until after the death of her four young children and her own severe illness that she began to see her need for a relationship with God and began to seek Him. Selina's conversion experience came at a time when revival was coming to England and from the beginning of her Christian walk she was ready to help the cause of Christ with her faithful witness, financial support, and influence.

209

Soon after her conversion, Selina developed friendships with both John and Charles Wesley and George Whitefield. Selina had power and influence and did not hesitate to use it for the good of revival. Being in her company opened many doors for these men, including opportunities to preach to the aristocracy and to gain financial backing for their work.

While her husband was a religious man, it doesn't appear that he was a Christian. Yet, he never interfered with Selina's newfound faith. It appears that he was sympathetic to the Christian cause and didn't hinder her work. However, it wasn't until after her husband's untimely death in 1746 that Selina was able to give herself fully to the work of the Lord and turn her full attention toward revival. She spoke of revival to everyone she had contact with and her witness spread widely, especially among the nobility. Even the King himself held Lady Huntingdon in high regard.

Selina not only devoted herself, her time, and her influence to God, but she also gave her incredible fortune to further the Lord's work. Her husband had left his vast fortune in her control and it is estimated that she gave many millions of dollars in her lifetime to furthering the spread of the Gospel. The Countess lived simply and sacrificially, selling her country homes, jewelry, and other trappings of the aristocracy, giving the proceeds of these sales to Christian work.

Lady Huntingdon humbly served the Lord by simply touching the lives of those with whom she came in contact with, giving of her time and her resources. Even at her death she thought of the welfare of others, bequeathing her entire estate to support Christian work. She gave herself to her Lord in both life and in death. Her last words were, "My work is done; I have nothing to do but go to my Father" (Hyde, *Story of Methodism,* p. 102).

Amy Carmichael
Founder of Dohnavur Fellowship

Amy Carmichael was an ordinary woman with extraordinary love for people. She was born in Ireland in 1867, the first child to Christian parents, David and Catherine Carmichael. Amy grew up in a large family, seven children in all. Her parents were deeply devoted to Christ and raised their children to love and serve God. She learned early on the discipline of sitting quietly and the importance of a total, unswerving commitment to Christ.

Amy was not pleased with her appearance. She had brown eyes, which she found very unattractive. While quite young, she remembered her mother's teaching that if she asked God anything, He would surely grant her request. So, having spiritual stirrings at a young age, Amy proceeded to ask God to change her eye color, not realizing that sometimes His answer is no. Much to her disappointment, they remained brown. But as the years unfolded, Amy came to realize the wisdom of God's denial of her request. While serving the Lord in India, those brown eyes served her well and made her fit for service where God had put her,

During her formative years, Amy became a very determined and well-disciplined girl. Her father had taught her to be "tough", teaching her never to give in to a difficulty. Due to her father encouraging her "tomboy" spirit, Amy learned to deal with physical stress and strain and developed the determination and an obedience to spiritual principles that gave her the vitality she would need to serve God on the mission field. Because of living in a large family, she also developed a tender heart and was sensitive to the needs of others.

As she grew into adulthood, Amy felt called to missions. She answered that call with great joy and went as a missionary to Japan. Next she went to China and then Ceylon (known as Sri Lanka). Finally, Amy was called to India where she served for over 50 years. It was here that she realized God's wisdom in His choice of her eye color. Nearly without exception, Indians had brown eyes. Amy's brown eyes and Indian dress made her more able to minister to women and girls in the field, appearing to them as one of their own.

After Amy had lived in India for some time, she continued to be concerned about a distressing situation that existed in most of the pagan temples of India. Young girls were taken in, many times only as children, and made temple prostitutes. The girls had a horrible existence and Amy became deeply grieved for them. She became convinced that she must help these young girls wanting to escape their horrible life in the temples. While living in Dohnavur, India, with a band of women that had been converted to Christ, Amy founded the Dohnavur Fellowship, which became a haven for homeless children, especially those girls who had escaped from temple prostitution. She was even given "temple babies", infants that were born of the temple prostitutes, to raise in her "home". While the Dohnavur fellowship began mainly as a haven for girls, later a home for boys was also built.

The Dohnavur Fellowship became Amy's all-consuming ministry, which she gave her life to, never even taking a furlough back to Europe. She wrote 35 books detailing her life in India that have been widely read in Christian circles and have inspired many to follow their call to the mission field. (Tucker, *Daughters,* p. 305).

Patricia R. Chadwick

Catherine Mumford Booth
Mother of the Salvation Army

At Christmas time, we are all familiar with the Salvation Army. Outside the local department stores and on several street corners we hear the ringing of the bells and the clinking of the change as it falls into Salvation Army Kettle. The Salvation Army is synonymous with charity and helping others less fortunate. Did you ever wonder how this organization got its start? It was founded by William and Catherine Booth, of London, England when local churches refused to care for the poor.

Catherine Mumford Booth was born the daughter of a coachbuilder in 1829 at Ashbourne, Derbyshire. When she was a child the family moved to Boston, Lincolnshire and later they lived at Brixton. Catherine was a devout Christian and by the time she was twelve, she had read the entire Bible eight times. She also had a social conscience.

When she was only twelve years old, Catherine became secretary to a little temperance society. She also raised money for sending the gospel to foreign land, even denying herself sugar in order to contribute to missions. She was a bright and earnest child and wrote articles for publication when she was very young. Catherine had a good heart and always took up the cause of the weak and unfortunate.

215

In 1852, Catherine met William Booth, a young Wesleyan preacher. William's father had once been wealthy, but had died, leaving his family penniless. William was working as an apprentice while preaching to support himself and his family. William and Catherine shared a strong commitment to social reform and while they were both poor, they joined heart and hand for soul saving and the uplifting of humanity. They were married at Stockwell New Chapel on June 16, 1855.

William became a circuit preacher, and later assistant pastor in a London church. He was a very successful evangelist and had many calls for him to speak in different parts of England. But his real love was evangelistic work, a work he shared with Catherine. When he was only 27, he was ordered by the conference to give up his evangelistic work and was given a small church to pastor. It was here that Catherine began to conduct classes and speak on temperance.

The Booths were next moved to a town of fifty thousand people. Their little church numbered less than 100 members when they began their ministry there, but soon the church was crowded with nearly two thousand people. This church became known as the "Converting Shop".

The stories of Catherine's assistance to the poor are both touching and thrilling. She was of a very sensitive nature and was really quite shy. She dreaded the thought of speaking in public, but felt that God had laid this upon her. So she began to preach and people responded. Hundreds of people were soon converted under her speaking. Her husband's health failed and she was compelled to take his place, which she did, and was a great success. Calls began to come for both her and her husband to hold evangelistic meetings, but the leadership of his church conference disapproved. At last the Booth's felt they must resign the conference and be free to go where God might call them.

The ministry of the Salvation Army originated in the slums of London, where William and Catherine held tent meetings and marched through the streets to advertise the meetings. From this humble beginning comes the great organization of the Salvation Army that is known worldwide.

Pundita Ramabai Sarvesvati
Bible Translator

Pundita Ramabai was fortunate in having a father who, contrary to all Hindu customs, believed in the education of women. Her father educated Ramabai's mother and so she inherited from both parents a love for learning. But so unpopular were the views of Ramada's father that, though himself a pundit (a learned man or teacher), he was obliged to withdraw into the jungles and take up his residence there. Here Ramabai was instructed by her father. She showed great aptitude and could repeat from memory 23,000 verses of Hindu Shastras.

When she was sixteen years of age, famine came to the land and for eleven days they lived on water and leaves. They left their jungle home and for some years the father was a wandering teacher. Father and mother died and she had only a brother to care for her. Ramabai became a lecturer, advocating the education of women and the repudiation of the custom of child marriages. Her learning attracted great attention. At Calcutta the punditi, or learned men, called her to appear before them. After a long examination, she passed with flying colors and received the title of Sarasvati (King, *Woman*, p. 460).

At the height of her success, her brother died. Now she was left without a male relative in India. However, six months later she was married to an educated Bengali man, though he was of a lower caste than her. But they had both thrown off Hindu beliefs.

After having been married for nineteen months, her husband died and Ramabai was again alone without a male relative. At this point she also had a baby girl to care for. She was now a widow, and what was a worse fate was that she was a widow with no son. This predicament was despised in India. All relatives also shunned her because she had broken caste by her marriage. But Ramabai faced the world again and began lecturing.

After a time, Pundita left her homeland and went to England. She had recently become a Christian, and spent much time studying the Bible in Sanskrit and then in English. In England she worked hard to perfect her English and after a time became professor of Sanskrit in the Ladies' College at Cheltenham. But all this time her heart was with the poor little child-widows of India. She was invited to come to America to attend the graduation of her cousin Joshee from a medical school in Philadelphia. Here Ramabai began a careful study of the public school system, believing she could apply the principals in India.

When Ramabai's training and plans were complete, she went back to India, determined to educate high-caste Hindu widows. In times of famine, child-widows were turned out to die or be picked up by surly men to lead them into a life of shame. Ramabai's wanted to rescue these girls. She opened a school and in 1898 she had 350 child-widows that had passed through the school. Fourteen had been trained as teachers, eight as nurses, seven as missionary assistants, and ten had homes of their own. In her school-home they became healthy and happy living in a new world of Christian love.

Patricia R. Chadwick

Fanny Crosby
Hymn Writer and Poet

Fanny J. Crosby was an American hymn writer and poet, writing over 9,000 hymns during her lifetime along with many secular songs, cantatas, and lyrical productions of various kinds. During the era of "gospel song" (1870-1920), Fanny Crosby's popular ballads reigned supreme. Her hymns are still sung today all over the world.

Fanny was born into a poor family in Putnam County, New York on May 24, 1820. She became ill as an infant, causing her eyes to inflame. Living in a small town where there was no doctor, the family was desperate for help. A stranger, claiming to be a doctor, treated Fanny, putting a police on her eyes, claiming it would draw the infection out. Instead, as her eyes cleared, white scar tissue began to form over her eyes, and Fanny was to remain blind the rest of her life. A few months later, Fanny's father fell ill and died.

These tragic events might have scarred most children for life, but it was not so for Fanny. Her mother had to find work, so she left Fanny with her grandmother, Eunice. Eunice was determined that Fanny wouldn't grow up to be helpless. She wanted the girl to learn to be independent and capable of supporting herself. Eunice verbally taught Fanny all about the world around her, describing her surroundings in great detail.

This led Fanny to have a great love of nature. She also required Fanny to exercise her mind by having her memorize the entire Bible, along with poetry of the day. This store of knowledge would help Fanny the rest of her life.

While she does not rank with the great poets of her day, her songs have reached many hearts where more stately productions would not have gained admittance. Her mission has been a noble one and well performed: "To rescue the perishing, care for the dying...tell them of Jesus, the mighty to save."

Her talent for writing verses showed itself when she was not more than eight years old, and every year since has seen something from her pen. All these have been written in her blindness and many of them, so full of joy and hope and light that it's hard to remember they were written in darkness.

Patricia R. Chadwick

Emeline Dryer
Christian Educator

While many have heard of D.L. Moody, the famous revivalist of the 19th century, and the prominent Bible School that bears his name, not many know of the woman who helped him make this school a success. Her name is Emeline Dryer.

Emeline Dryer, or Emma, as her friends knew her, was born in Massachusetts in 1835. While she was still a child, both her parents died, leaving her orphaned. Emma was sent to live with an aunt in New York State and there she found educational opportunities open to her that were beyond the norm for a rural New Yorker. Being an excellent student, Emma gladly pursued her studies. She went on to study at the LeRoy Female Seminary and graduated with Highest Honors.

After she graduated, Emma joined the staff of Knoxville Female College and stayed on there until the Civil War. For the next few years, Emma taught elementary school and then accepted an offer to join the faculty of Illinois State Normal University in 1864. Throughout her teaching career, Emma displayed a deep commitment to Christ. She often spent her summers and holidays participating in Christian work, such as teaching, evangelizing, discipleship, and relief-work.

In 1870, Emma went through a trial that would change her direction in life. In that year she became ill with typhoid fever. Her doctors did not hold out much hope that she'd ever recover and Emma, herself, didn't expect to live through the illness. But the Lord had other plans. He provided complete healing and through this trial in her life, Emma felt God's call to commit her life to Christian service rather than secular teaching.

It was not an easy decision for her to enter full-time Christian work. As head of the women's faculty at Illinois State Normal University, she received a good salary, security, and much respect. To enter full-time Christian service meant for her to give this all up. But after counting the costs, she followed God's lead and in late 1870, Emma moved to Chicago for a position that offered no salary and no worldly recognition. Miss Dryer was now going to live by faith. It was during this year that Emma was introduced to D.L. Moody and his wife, Emma, and they became fast friends.

While Mr. Moody admired Emma's deep faith, he saw even more in her than that. He saw a woman of high intelligence, with superb teaching skills and a deep, practical knowledge of Scripture. Whatever Emma set her mind to, she accomplished. Time proved her to be dependable, energetic, and dedicated to Christian work.

In 1871, after the terrible fire that devastated Chicago, Moody began to spend most of his time ministering to the needs of those damaged financially and physically by the fire. He invited all the youth to his Church and he had enlisted the help of Emma Dryer to teach the masses of people Bible Study classes. He was able to persuade Emma to remain in Chicago and continue with her teaching at the Moody Church. He also prompted Emma to work as the head of Chicago's Women's Aid Society and as superintendent of the Women's Auxiliary of the YMCA (later know as the YWCA). Seeing how this work was growing fueled Moody's interest educational purposes. He began to develop a plan in which those men and women entering upon mission or evangelistic work might receive systematic training in the Bible.

In early 1873, a few months before He was to return to England on an evangelistic campaign, Moody convinced Emma Dryer to open a school to train women who wanted to enter home or foreign missions or evangelistic work. This school would give needed training in Bible, theology, and practically ministry to fulfill Moody's primary goal of getting trained women evangelists and personal workers into the homes of unchurched residents of Chicago. While the school began with training women, Moody had a much larger vision and intended it to eventually include men as well.

With the influence of D.L. Moody, the school was provided with proper funding to support Emma and the women in training. The school provided suitable training befitting those going into Christian work. It was from these humble beginnings that the Chicago Bible Institute (later known as Moody Bible Institute) was born.

In 1883, with the permission of Moody, Emma organized and headed weekly prayer meetings known as the "May

Institute". At these meetings church members would meet to pray and have open discussions in regards to the Bible and the work of the Church. Emma was especially interested in deepening the role of women in the Christian community, as well as in their own families. It was with this goal in mind that she led a ladies Bible Study where she urged women to take an active role in their children's education and upbringing. She urged them on into Christian service so they would be an example to their children of serving Christ in their community.

Emma Dryer gave her life in service to her God. She gave up a life of financial security and worldly acclaim to live a life based on her faith in God to provide for her needs while she strove to further the work of His kingdom. God did faithfully provide for her during her entire life and developed her work into a lasting legacy that continues even today in training men and women for the work of Christian service: the Moody Bible Institute.

Patricia R. Chadwick

Susannah Spurgeon
Founder of the Book Fund

While Susannah Spurgeon will always be remembered as the faithful wife and encourager of the great preacher Charles Haddon Spurgeon, she deserves recognition in her own right by the Christian Church in connection with her fund for supplying theological books to clergymen and ministers too poor to buy them. The importance of this Christian work should not be overlooked or underestimated. At the time in which Mrs. Spurgeon lived, many ministers living in England were given such a poor wage that they could barely feed their families, let alone buy books to help them grow spiritually and improve their ministries. In fact, when the Book Fund was started it was discovered that many ministers had not been able to buy a new book for ten years!

Mrs. Spurgeon was born Susannah Thompson on January 15, 1832 to Mr. and Mrs. R.B. Thompson in the Southern suburbs of the City of London. She was raised in a godly home and had earnest Christian friends as she grew up and she herself became a Christian as a young girl. But since, in those days, there were not many organizations or churches that encouraged young believers to pursue Christian service or further their knowledge of God, there was a coldness and indifference common to the youth of that day, Susannah included.

In 1852, Susannah saw for the first time the man that was to become her beloved husband. He was a mere youth of 19 and had been asked to preach in the famous Park Street Chapel in London and at the insistence of her friends she attended the service. At this point in her life, Susannah had grown so spiritually cold that she didn't understand the clear Gospel preaching of this young man and she was not impressed with his preaching.

When C.H. Spurgeon finally accepted the pastorate of New Park Street Chapel, Miss Thompson often saw him at the home of her dear friends Mr. and Mrs. Olney who were members of the church. Though they saw each other often, neither Mr. nor Mrs. Spurgeon remembers their first introduction. It appears that it didn't take long for Susannah to get over her prejudices regarding Charles as a preacher and she soon realized her Christian life was far from what it should be. Mr. Spurgeon soon heard of Susannah's desire to improve her Christian walk and gave her and illustrated copy of "The Pilgrim's Progress" to help her along that path. She was very impressed by his concern for her and from that time on their friendship grew and it wasn't long that it blossomed into love (Ray, *Mrs. C.H. Spurgeon,* p. 30). Charles and Susannah were married on January 8, 1856.

On September 20, 1856, Susannah gave birth to a set of twin boys in her New Kent Road home. She remained weak for some time after the birth of her sons and, though she eventually recovered, she never again gained full and robust health. Much of Susannah's life was spent suffering from physical ailments that kept her bedridden for long periods of time.

Although weak and ailing much of her adult life, Susannah was a faithful trainer of her two sons in Christian doctrine and she had the joy of seeing them both become Christians at an early age. When they became grown men, both of her boys publicly recognized how much the influence of their mother's example and teaching played a part in their conversion.

Charles Spurgeon was a prolific writer and had most of his sermons published. In the summer of 1875 he completed the first volume of *Lectures to my Students* and he gave his wife a proof copy of the book, asking for her opinion. She told her husband that she wished she could place that volume in the hands of every minister in England. To that her husband replied, "Then why not do so: how much will you give?" (Ray, *Mrs. C.H. Spurgeon,* p. 67).

Susannah was not prepared for his question, but it challenged her to see if she could spare the money from her housekeeping or personal account to fulfill her wish. At that time she remembered some money that she had put away whenever she had some extra. She went to her room and got the money and when it was counted she realized that she had enough money to pay for one hundred copies of the work. It was in that instant that the **Book Fund** was born.

The next issue of *The Sword and the Trowel*, a magazine which was put out by her husband, contained an announcement of Mrs. Spurgeon's intention of giving out the books and inviting poor Baptist ministers to apply for the book. The applications proved more numerous than she anticipated and in that first distribution she gave out two hundred copies instead of the one hundred she originally proposed. In the following issue of his publication, Charles told of the many ministers desiring new books to increase their knowledge and improve their ministries and of the **Book Fund** that Susannah created to fulfill these needs. Money began to come in to finance the **Book Fund** so that books could be provided to needy ministers.

Susannah continued the work of the **Book Fund** for the rest of her life. Her last thoughts before her death were for the **Book Fund**, and for the poor ministers who were benefited by its aid. In her will she left a sum of money for the assistance of the work.

Besides the support she gave her husband in his ministry, the time she spent raising and training her boys, and the work she did with the **Book Fund**, Susannah Spurgeon gave a good deal of time to literary work. Her most treasured work was "C.H. Spurgeon's Autobiography, compiled from his Diary, Letters, and Records". As a writer, Susannah had a rare literary gift. She wrote several books in her lifetime including *Ten Years of My Life in the Service of the Book Fund*, *Ten Years After*, and several devotional books.

If greatness is determined by the amount of good a person does in the world, if it is only another name for unselfish devotion in the service of others, then Susannah Spurgeon go down in history as one of the greatest women of her time.

Joni Eareckson Tada
Founder of Joni & Friends Ministry

Joni Eareckson Tada is a remarkable woman. Injured in a diving accident at the age of 17, Joni has had to endure more physical suffering than most of us ever will. Though she suffered a deep depression and lost the will to live in the aftermath of her accident, she gradually came back to a deeper relationship with God. Because of her early struggles, she has become strong in her faith and is a testimony to the world of how when we are weak, God is strong. Her story is not one of bitterness and despair, as we might imagine it to be, but one of love and victory.

Joni Eareckson Tada was born in Baltimore, Maryland in 1950 to John and Lindy Eareckson. She was the youngest of four sisters, Linda, Jay, and Kathy. Her name is pronounced "Johnny", being he named after her father. Joni inherited her father's athletic and creative abilities, giving father and daughter a special bond. Her childhood was an extremely happy one. She grew into a young adult surrounded by love, happiness, and security in her parent's home. The Eareckson family shared a great love for the outdoors, which promoted family togetherness. They shared in various outdoor activities such as camping trips, horseback riding, hiking, tennis, and swimming.

In 1967, after graduating from high school, Joni had her fateful accident. It was a hot July day and she was to meet her

231

sister Kathy and some friends at the beach on Chesapeake Bay to swim. When she arrived, she dove in quickly, and immediately knew something was wrong. Though she felt no real pain, tightness seemed to encompass her. Her first thought was that she was caught in a fishing net and she tried to break free and get to the surface. Panic seized her as she realized she couldn't move and she was lying face down on the bottom of the bay. She realized she was running out of air and resigned herself to the fact that she was going to drown.

Her sister, Kathy, called for her. She ran to Joni and pulled her up. To Kathy's surprise, Joni could not support herself and tumbled back into the water. Kathy pulled her out and Joni gasped for air. Joni was puzzled as to why her arms were still tied to her chest. Then to her dismay, Joni realized they were not tied, but were draped lifelessly across her sister's back. Kathy yelled for someone to call an ambulance and Joni was rushed to the hospital.

Joni's life was changed forever that July day in 1967. She had broken her neck - a fracture between the fourth and fifth cervical levels. She was now a quadriplegic, paralyzed from the shoulders down. While her friends were busy preparing to go to college in the fall, Joni was fighting for her very life and having to accept the fact that she would have to live out the rest of her life in a wheelchair.

Joni's rehabilitation was not easy. As you might imagine she was angry and she raged against her fate. She struggled with depression and often times she wanted to end her life. She could not understand how God could let this happen to her. Before the accident she had felt that she wasn't living the life she should be so she had prayed that God would change

232

Patricia R. Chadwick

her life - that He'd turn it around. After months of staring at the ceiling and wallowing in her depression, Joni began to wonder if this was God's answer to her prayer.

This realization that God was working in her life was the beginning of Joni's journey to wholeness as a disabled person. She participated in various rehabilitation programs that taught her how to live with her disabilities and she immersed herself in God's Word to become spiritually strong.

Joni's life has been a full one. She learned early on to compensate for her handicaps. Being naturally creative, she learned to draw and paint holding her utensils with her teeth. She began selling her artwork and the endeavor was a great success. There was a real demand for her work. She kept herself very busy with her artwork and gained for herself a degree of independence. She was also able to share Christ's love in her drawings. She always signed her paintings "PTL" which stood for "Praise the Lord".

Joni has also become a sought after conference speaker, author, and actress, portraying herself in the World Wide Pictures production of *Joni*, the life story of Joni Eareckson in 1978. She has written several books including *Holiness in Hidden Places*, *Joni*, which was her autobiography, and many children's titles. Her most satisfying and far-reaching work, however, is her advocacy on behalf of the disabled (Hosier, *100 Christian Women*, p. 240).

In 1979, Joni moved to California to begin a ministry to the disabled community around the globe. She called it *Joni and Friends Ministries* (**JAF Ministries**), fulfilling the mandate of Jesus in Luke 14:13,23 to meet the needs of the poor, crippled, and lame. Joni understood first-hand the loneliness and alienation many handicapped people faced and their need for friendship and salvation. The ministry was soon immersed with calls for both physical and spiritual help for the disabled.

JAF Ministries thus uncovered the vast hidden needs of the disabled community and began to train the local church for effective outreach to the disabled, an often-overlooked mission field. **JAF Ministries** today includes local offices in such major cities as Charlotte, Chicago, Dallas/Fort Worth, Phoenix, and San Francisco. The goal of the ministry is to have ten such offices in metropolitan areas by the year 2001.

Through **JAF Ministries**, Joni tapes a five-minute radio program called *Joni and Friends*, heard daily all over the world. She has heart for people who, like herself, must live with disabilities. Her role as an advocate for the disabled has led to a presidential appointment to the National Council on Disability for over three years. Joni also serves on the board of the Lausanne Committee for World Evangelization as a senior associate for evangelism among disabled persons. Joni has also begun Wheels for the World, a ministry that involves restoring wheelchairs and distributing them in developing nations.

Joni has won many awards and commendations throughout her life. In 1993 she was named **Churchwoman of the Year** by the Religious Heritage Foundation and the National Association of Evangelicals named her **Layperson of the Year**, making her the first woman ever to receive that honor. Also among the numerous awards she has received are the **American Academy of Achievement's Golden Plate**

Award, The Courage Award of the Courage Rehabilitation Center, the **Award of Excellence** from the Patricia Neal Rehabilitation Center, the **Victory Award** from the National Rehabilitation Hospital, and the **Golden Word Award** from the International Bible Society (Hosier, *100 Christian Women*, p. 240).

In 1982, Joni married Ken Tada. Today, eighteen years later, the marriage is strong and committed and they are still growing together in Christ. Ken and Joni travel together with JAF Ministries speaking at family retreats about the day-to-day experiences of living with disabilities. At the helm of **JAF Ministries**, Ken and Joni strive to demonstrate in tangible ways that God has not abandoned those with disabilities. And they speak from experience.

Anne Graham Lotz
Bible Teacher/Conference Teacher

Anne Graham Lotz is a third-generation Christian who has wholeheartedly given herself in service to God. She is a gifted communicator, with excellent abilities in speaking, writing, and teaching the Bible. Anne's message is clear and simple as she calls people to a personal relationship with God through His Word. Her mission in life is to make God's Word personal and relevant to ordinary people. And she's meeting with great success.

Anne has a great spiritual heritage. She was born in May of 1948 to the Rev. Billy and Ruth Bell Graham. Along with her parents, both sets of grandparents were faithful Christians. While it is true that her father was absent much of the time, Anne never grew up resenting him for this. In fact, she was not even aware of what a great man her father was. To her he was just "Daddy". She knew he was gone a lot, but to the family this was normal. She and her 4 siblings led a sheltered life, her parents wisely shielding them from the scrutiny and exploitation of the press. Her childhood home was in the mountains of North Carolina and she grew up in a very "ordinary" atmosphere. Since her father was gone quite often, most of her childhood was spent under the godly influence of her mother Ruth and her maternal grandmother, Virginia Bell.

236

As a teenager, Anne found herself in a personal crisis, feeling inferior and continually striving to find her niche in a home where, in her eyes, her parents were "spiritual giants" and her siblings more gifted than she. She also felt the pressure of living up to other people's expectations. Much was expected from "Billy Graham's daughter". It was when she decided to live her life to please God alone that she felt peace in her life.

Anne was married at the young age of 18 to Dan Lotz and has been happily married for 33 years. They live in North Carolina and have three grown children: Jonathan, Morrow, and Rachel-Ruth. It was during her days as a young mother that God cultivated the gift of Bible teaching in her life. As a young mother, she struggled to make God's Word meaningful in her own life. While she had the fine example of her mother to follow, Anne still struggled to make God's Word a consistent, vital part of her life. She prayed that God would help her to learn to study the Bible and make it relevant to her.

He answered her prayer by giving Anne the opportunity to become involved in Bible Study Fellowship (BSF). With her husband's encouragement, Anne became a teacher for BSF and this experience laid the groundwork in Biblical study that she had longed for. This experience with BSF also brought to her the realization of her spiritual gifts of teaching and Bible exposition. In 1976 she established BSF in Raleigh and the class immediately had five hundred in attendance, with a waiting list. She continued to teach for 12 years without ever missing a class. During that time, the class multiplied eightfold.

Because of her commitment to BSF, Anne declined many invitations to speak. Though she continued to refuse the requests for her to lecture, invitations kept coming. She began to sense God's call into an itinerant ministry of Bible teaching/preaching. Anne followed that call and left BSF and began a nonprofit organization called **AnGel Ministries** in 1988.

AnGel Ministries under girds the ministry God has called Anne to. She created the name by taking her initials, AGL and adding the "n" and the "e" in between to form the word "angel". She did this because of her belief in the ministry of angels in the Bible. Anne's belief is that angels were messengers of God, never going anywhere except where God sent them, never speaking unless they gave out God's Word, and only addressing those whom God placed in front of them. To her, this described her ministry perfectly because it was her commitment to go wherever God would send her and to speak His Word to whomever He would place in front of her.

Anne has had to work through some crucial challenges in her ministry, but they've given her a deeper understanding of the challenges that women in ministry have to face. One such challenge happened when she was asked to speak at a pastors' conference. Many of those in attendance didn't agree with the idea of women teaching men and during that conference dozens of pastors in attendance stood up and turned their backs to her. This experience led her to examine her sense of call from God and she prayed fervently and intensely searched the Scriptures for an answer. God confirmed her call through several Scripture passages, one of which is found in Jeremiah 1:17: "Therefore prepare yourself and arise, and speak to them all that I command you. Do not be dismayed before their faces". She good-naturedly states, "Only God was telling me not to be afraid of their backs". She felt God was telling her to stand up and say whatever He told her to. She was, after all, only accountable to God, not her audience. Though she fully accepts her ministry as God's call on her life, Anne is careful not to offend anyone when she speaks. She only goes where she is invited and never assumes any authority over her audience. She believes her only authority is the authority of God's Word (Hosier, *100 Christian Women*, p.102).

Over the years, Anne has used **Angel Ministries** as a vehicle for presenting God's Word in a relevant, personal way to ordinary people through live presentations, tapes, and books. **AnGel Ministries** currently provides an international/national speaking and tape ministry, devotional study books, and a twice-yearly newsletter. Today Anne continues to follow God's call as (in her own words) a "traveling missionary". She is in great demand as a speaker worldwide and is actively pursuing her life's mission of bringing God's Word to a needy world.

Bibliography

About.com, "Women's Voices: Quotations From Women", database online. Available at http://www.about.com, 2000.

Adelman, Joseph, *Famous Women*, New York, Ellis M. Lonow Company, 1926.

Bolton, Sarah, *Famous Leaders Among Women*, Boston, Thomas Crowell & Company, 1895.

Hosier, Helen Kooiman, *100 Christian Women Who Changed the World*, Grand Rapids, MI, Flemming H. Revell, 2000.

Hyde, A.B., *The Story of Methodism*, Springfield, Mass., Willey & Company, 1869.

Jackson, Guida M., *Women Who Ruled the World*, New York, Barnes & Noble, 1990.

James, Edward T., Janet James and Paul S. Boyer, eds., *Notable American Women*, vol. 1, Belknap Harvard, 1971.

James, Edward T., Janet James and Paul S. Boyer, eds., Notable *American Women*, vol. 2, Belknap Harvard, 1971.

James, Edward T., Janet James and Paul S. Boyer, eds., *Notable American Women*, vol. 3, Belknap Harvard, 1971.

Janney, Rebecca Price, *Great Women in American History,* Camp Hill, PA, Horizon Books, 1996.

King, William C., *Woman,* Chicago, Illinois, The King-Richardson Company, 1903.

Lumpkin, Katharine DuPre, *The Emancipation of Angelina Grimké,* Chapel Hill North Carolina, the University of North Carolina Press, 1974.

Patron, James, *Eminent Women of the Age,* Hartford, CT, S.M. Betts & Company, 1869.

Ray, Charles, *Mrs. C.H. Spurgeon,* St. John, Indiana, Christian Book Gallery, 1903.

Tucker, Ruth and Walter Liefeld, *Daughters of the Church,* Grand Rapids, MI, Zondervan, 1987.

Wheeler, Noelle, ed., *Daughters of Destiny,* Bulverde, Texas, Mantle Ministries, 2000.

To order additional copies of

History's
Women

Send $15.95 plus $3.95 shipping and
handling to:

P.C. Publications
22 William St.
Batavia, NY 14020

For credit card orders visit:
http://www.HistorysWomen.com
or call or fax (716)343-2810

*Quantity discounts available